INSPIRED BY GOD

TESTIMONIES OF A BLOODWASHED SORCERER REVEALING THE THREE CRUCIFIED JESUSES

BY SPAIRMORE LEE SMITH

Inspired By God
Testimony of a Bloodwashed Sorcerer Revealing the Three Crucified Jesuses

By Spairmore Lee Smith

ISBN: 978-0-692-09478-5

Published by: ShoCott Enterprises, LLC

ShoCott Enterprises
Collaboration Is King

ShoCott Enterprises, LLC
P.O. Box 5323
Tel: (717) 802-0010
Email: ShoCottEnterprises@gmail.com
Website: www.ShoCottEnterprises.com

Unless otherwise indicated, Bible quotations are taken from The King James Version

Table of Contents

Dedication

This book is dedicated unto Almighty God! The Holy Spirit is responsible for guiding me in every way inside this book. My limited education couldn't have figured out or discern the hidden things of Almighty God.

Matthew 11:25. At that time Jesus answered and said, I thank thee, O Father, Lord of heaven and earth, because thou hast hid these things from the wise and prudent, and hast revealed them unto babes.

In 2010, I was instructed by The Holy Spirit to write. when I began to write, everything seemed like garbage at the time, why? The spirits of witchcrafts were still upon me. I can recall showing Pastor James this book and he laughed me to scorn. But after being totally delivered in 2012, God open the eyes of my heart and I was able to see what was written therein. All glory unto Go, in the name of Jesus Christ of Nazareth.

Acknowledgements

First, I acknowledge God for using a dump like me to bring these revelations unto His people! God, I thank you in the name of Jesus Christ of Nazareth, Amen.

The Publisher is also grateful to the following for their permission to use their names in this book:

Prophetess Shonyah Hawkins-Cottman, from Pennsylvania, USA whom God used to edit "His words to life". All glory to Our Lord and Savior in the mighty name of Jesus Christ of Nazareth.

The author is also grateful to the following persons, for their editorial advice:

Mr. Cyril Lebert, my former Principal and the only "father figure" I had at age fourteen, while attending the Pembroke Hall Secondary School, Ken Hill Drive Kingston 20. Jamaica WI.

Bishop Stanley Ivey, consulting editor of this book and Pastor of the Blackwoods New Testament and the Thompson Town New Testament Church, in Clarendon Jamaica WI.

Nicholas Webb from Kinston 13, Jamaica for designing the book cover.

Foreword

I salute and commend Bro Spairmore Lee Smith for being honest, bold and extremely forthright in sharing his testimony in this book. He placed his life and history plainly for every reader to know that God can save anyone who hears His voice and repents. Jesus Christ of Nazareth is emphasized throughout his testimony as Lord, Savior and Deliverer. This book is a must read for all who are Christian today, especially those struggling with witchcraft and balm yard activities and curses. It will be difficult to put down once you start reading it.

Spairmore will take you where he was as a former sorcerer and what it did to him for twenty-two years. He will explain why the church today needs to have spiritual discernment like never before, because of how Satan and his deception has taken over many places of worship today. You will understand very clearly why so many churches, have so little positive impact, as he explains the three Jesuses that control the spirit realm and different churches today.

Spairmore took his readers through his personal deliverance and how the reader can be delivered and remain free. He clearly explained how Satan blinded the minds of many who attend churches today believing they are doing God's will and work. You will learn the reason and solution for pride and sexual immorality in churches today and the need for each believer to study the bible for him or herself.

Spairmore candidly tackled the problem of divorce while elevating and restoring women to their rightful place within the Church of Jesus Christ of Nazareth. He provided many warnings to: Bishops, Pastors, Preachers, Prayer Warriors and everyone who is called a Christian or Christian worker. Read and pray, pray and read, because your life will not be the same once you read this book.

Bishop Stanley Ivey,
Pastor and District Overseer,
Blackwoods and Thompson Town
New Testament Church of God,
Clarendon JWI

Introduction

This book contains my testimony, a former sorcerer; who is now a blood washed believer. I will be revealing to you my reader, the three crucified Jesuses and the three different Jesuses that operate from the three spiritual realms. This book will enable all readers to come to grips with the real spiritual situations that we are facing inside our Churches today. In this book, I try to expose readers to the wealth of ideas and concepts related to many aspects of everyday life inside our churches. This book will encourage everyone to learn about their own spiritual rights inside the spirit realms. This book further encourages the readers to study God's word, so they will be able to defend themselves against Satan and his army. There is a deliberate broadening of the range of testimonies to which readers are exposed inside our churches that need answers and clarification.

Additionally, the language used in this book is easy for the average readers. The numerous testimonies offer exercises of all types. There is work for both readers and Church to repair the breaches or damages incurred in our relationship with Almighty God over the years. I do hope that this information will help everyone in their personal walk with God, In the name of Jesus Christ of Nazareth.

The chapter sequence covers when I was being exposed unto "falling angels inside of The Church!" When I was taught how to work and communicate with the graveyard demons and

1

how I was persecuted for calling on the name of "Jesus Christ of Nazareth". There will be encouraging words for young converts and Prophets on how to obey the Holy Spirit. Chapter Five focuses primarily on empowering our women to preached and teach the undiluted gospel of Jesus Christ of Nazareth. You will also learn to identify your greatest enemy as a believer. For those who are married or divorced or desire to be married, learn how much marriages are honorable before Almighty God.

As a believer, we all need to learn about your spiritual rights and about the three Jesuses that were crucified and the three different stages of spiritual Deliverance. The book will end with the prayer that The Holy Spirit taught me. I know you will be empowered reading and knowing your spiritual rights.

Chapter One

Exposed to Fallen Angels

My name is Spairmore Lee Smith, I am a Jamaican by birth, and this is my true testimony! I was only four years old when I witnessed my father throwing a pot of boiling water on my mother. The boiling water ran from her breast to her stomach as she screamed in agony! My parents were arguing about something and to be honest, I don't really remember what they were arguing about. All I remember from that moment were the screams of my mother in agony, as I watched her covered with the boiling water over her body. My mother had been severely burned and my father was running away.

As the years progressed, I came to understand that the reason for the argument that day was the fact that my own father was molesting his sister! My mother knew about it and was leaving him. You see my mother caught them having sex. He burned my mother with hot water because she told his mother what was going on between him and his sister. It is believed that the molestation began when my father's sister was only six years old. "The Lord is slow to anger and abundant in loving kindness, forgiving iniquity (sin) and transgression; but He will by no means clear the guilty, visiting the iniquity (sin) of the fathers on the children to the third and fourth generation (Numbers 14:18)."

3

Inspired by God

The devil thought that he had me bound, with this and other generational curses. Well, I refused to accept responsibility for my father's actions and poor choices! I'm so glad that all these and all other generational curses were washed away, and I am now cleansed by the crucified Blood of The Lamb, Jesus Christ of Nazareth! I Declare and Decree, while Proclaiming and Pronouncing Victory! "VICTORY" over the enemy, in the mighty matchless name of Jesus Christ of Nazareth!

It was 1979 and Jamaica was about to hold their annual general election in a few weeks, according to surveys this election was expected to be a bloody one. A few weeks before the election, there was an incident that took place in the area where we lived. My mother was outside washing our clothes, she did not see what happened, but knew something did occur. A few days later individuals who thought my mother witnessed the event, paid us a visit. These men in an effort to keep my mother silent threatened my sister and me. I was told by my mother that a gun was placed inside my mouth as one of the criminals threatened to rape my three-year-old sister. All of this was done to scare my mother into keeping silent to cover up the crime they thought she witnessed.

My mother feared for our safety after that awful ordeal. Having no one to turn to and no one she thought to go to in the area, she moved us from Kingston Jamaica, to a district called York Town in the parish of Clarendon to my paternal grandmother. Shortly after arriving, it was clear that we were not really welcome there. You see, we were recognized or labelled the black sheep of the Barretts' family because we were Smiths'. We were considered the outcast of the family. We watched my mother leave us with eyes full of tears. I remember hearing her say, "I'll be back, mind your grandmother!" Our mother kept her promises. Each weekend we would see her, she brought food, clothing and other things we needed while staying with or grandmother. My God, they were difficult times. This happened for three long years, if she couldn't find the time, then she would send someone with items for us. Two years had passed since anyone had seen or heard anything from our mother. Isn't it ironic that whenever people need help, they find you, but when you need help they cannot be found! These people knew where our mother was, but no one took the time-out to see what was going with her.

After two years, our mother mysteriously turned up and revealed that her delay in uniting our family was due to her sister in Canada. You see my mom took ill in 1984 out of the blue. She would remain so, until 1986. Now even though she was ill, she would still try to visit us using money she set aside for us, from working. One afternoon, my mother arrived to find me at the river-side. I was later told that the reason for her visit that day was to explain what had happened to her. My Aunt Doris had sent for my mother to come to Canada. You see, my mother took care of my aunt's children while she was making a home for them in Canada. To show her appreciation, Aunt Doris had sent for her to come to

Canada. Now, my mother's girlfriend knew of my mother's plans to leave Jamaica with us. She did not want her to leave so she devised a plan to ask my mother for money. This woman was no friend of my mother. She borrowed money from my mom, the same money sent to my mother for traveling, was the same money we believe was used to obtain the service of an "Obeah man" or local voodoo priest. It was believed that he cast a spell that caused my mother to fall ill. The spirit of madness and spiritual depression had befallen her and she would walk the streets of Kingston for two years.

My mother told me years later that one day, while she was walking on the road one Sabbath morning she came across a church. She went inside and requested prayer; this is what people that are ill are instructed to do! She was weary and in need of healing. As she ventured into the church, she was met by a team of men who took their neckties off and began to bind her hands and feet and then called the police. In agony and despair, she cried out to God, that he would show these men her illness, that he would allow them to see the spiritual forces behind this madness that had crept in, so that she could be healed. As she began to petition God, there was an immediate rain fall that took place. The beating of heavy drops from heaven permeated the atmosphere. They were sent to cleanse the pain and suffering of an old woman whose rose was yet in full bloom. A kind gentle soul, one in that needed the deepest cleaning one could possibly receive from God. At that moment, her weakest moment, God granted her relief. He sent the rain, it fell steadily amid the sunny summer sky. It was after this cleansing began, the police were called. Yes, the church had called for the authorities, not knowing what was going on with my mother. After a while the police arrived at the church. At this time, the church finally understood and began to pray for my mother. But physically it was too late for my mother as the police were carting her off to the Mental Hospital for observation and treatment. What everyone failed to realize in those moments, before the authorities arrived, was that God had already begun his work in her. She wailed and cried for intervention from God, and he did show up on her behalf. She was finally broken and needed the hand of God to reach down and remove the years of doubt, bewilderment, and turmoil. My mother received from God what she needed spiritually that day. Two weeks my mother spent in that facility, one of the children of Aunt Doris, named Grace, visited my mother. My mother explained to her that she was not mentally ill, that she had a break down, it was an intervention and restoration from God. It was at that moment that Grace understood that she was there to do for my mother what no physical person could do, set her free! Grace signed my mother out of that facility. A cleansing of the mind, the heart, and the soul is what God had granted her.

My mother was now free from this place but had nowhere to go! Unable to stay with Grace who was staying with someone else at the time, my mother was now homeless. She was taken in by one of her cousin named Curtis, God bless his soul! This allowed my mother to have a steady, consistent place to call home for a while. Yet another manifestation that God knows what's best for us! We just need to trust his process. My mother during this time had an encounter with a man at a bus stop. This man came to her at a time when she needed a visitation from God. She had a vision that she would meet this man. Entering her presence, she knew it was God answering her prayers once again. You see, it was through this man, that my mother was led to this church where God would heal her; she attended this church for years.

Now that our mother was better and working again, we would expect to see her every two weeks. She came faithfully bearing food, clothing, toys, and money for us to attend school. But little did she know most of this was spent on the other children, as my sister and I were left at home doing chores. I was now working as their butler and my sister their house-maid. My mother was not aware at the time, but when she found how we were being treated and neglected, she was beyond angry. She couldn't believe that such blatant disregard for her young children by their own family, my father family, could take place. My mother has never forgotten those times, even unto this day. My mother carries with her the guilt of what was done to us because she was the one who placed us with those people. It is the prayer of my heart that God will grant her the wisdom to know that she has

8

been forgiven, as God had already forgiven and blot out all those trespasses against her!

Those times were difficult for me as a young boy; I can only imagine what it must have been like for my sister. Most of my days were spent by the river side trying to catch fish, crayfish, while stealing yams, and bananas from other fields, to feed myself. To be honest, I don't even remember anything good happening to me when I was with my grandmother in Clarendon. Somehow it seems that I blocked out many of my experiences. By the age of ten all I can recalled was being cursed by my grandmother, aunts, uncles, and cousins all of whom had no trouble letting us know how isolated we were from their family. I took to the streets, sleeping on the dirt floor of a make shift shanty among the homeless, in lieu of receiving beatings with hoses and electric wires, sometimes for no reason. I earned my wages at an early age, I became a handyman, earning money planting gardens and sold Ackee and the like. But my main meal was sugar cane all year round as this was there throughout the year. I can recall receiving a beating so bad by "Uncle Joe" with an electric wire one day. Now, this man was not even related to me. I found out after a few years had passed, he beat me out of hatred for my grandmother and father. It is believed that my grandmother was the one responsible for his father leaving his mother! He said that my grandmother "took his father away from his family" and I was the one who had to pay for something I didn't know about.

9

Inspired by God

By the time I was fourteen years old, I was a loose cannon, out of control! I turned to a local street gang and begin hanging with them, they were my family. By this time my birth family in Clarendon, were all afraid of me. So much damage was now done; my aunt took me back to my mother in Kingston and said to her, "He is your problem now!" It was during this time, at this age of fourteen, my mother learned from my older sister that I could not read. I was raised in the country by my father's family and received a raw deal. They worked me every day and every night as a handyman to feed the other children, while they were at school; no schooling, no education was offered to me. When I became rebellious, they would lock me outside the house and beat me near death with hose and electric wire or anything they could find. The beatings were so fierce I remember many times praying for death, or even to grow up overnight. This was my life for ten years while I was living in Clarendon.

January 1989, my sister and I were enrolled in the Pembroke Hall Secondary School. I can still recall that morning when I was given a book by the Assistant Principal to read. My God! I was just standing there staring inside the book without a word out my mouth, then Mr. Lebert the principal entered the office. "Mr. Lebert," the Assistant Principal shouted, "Here is another one that cannot read." Then the principal, who I later learned was Mr. Cyril Lebert, told the assistant, "Find a class and place him." "But we are full," she replied, "Just placed him where." Then Mr. Lebert gave us a stern warning, "Do not come here and waste your time like others," then he went inside his own office. God used, Mr. Cyril Lebert to place me strategically inside the physical realm, while He God: dealt with me from the spiritual realms!!!!

One Sunday morning, after I moved back with my mother in Kingston, she invited me to her church, Yes, the same church that the man she encountered from her vision led her to years prior. This was my first encounter with God! My mother's Bishop called me to the altar and told me to ask God for all what I wanted. "Lord!" I cried, "Please teach me how to read!" I didn't know God yet, but I needed help and I needed help fast. I started to attend Sunday school very regularly and began to become a fluent reader of the Bible after two years. God gave me a miracle! All I had to do was just ask! He taught me how to read in just a short time. I continued to ask God, to show up while I was on my knees at that altar that day, and He gave me Deuteronomy 4:29, "but if from thence thou shalt seek the Lord thy God, thou shalt find him, if thou seek him with all thy heart and with all thy soul." The spiritual realm was open to me. One Easter break holiday, the church had decided for all the church to visit Browns Town: this village is called Watt-Town and there every wizard and witch had to attend to become a certified sorcerer. This place is known as Jerusalem school room. During this visit it was prophesied over my life that there was a mantle given to me by God, belonging to

Elisha. I was told that I should go on a fasting for ten days. It was after these ten days of fasting, that I recognized the spiritual realm had opened to me. I had been certified as a Prophet of God, ordained to be God's mount piece for future use!

While I attended this church, I started to feel the heaviness in my spirit as if someone had placed his foot on my head. I began to accept this feeling on my forehead because I thought it was God communicating with me; but little did I know the spirit realm was now fully open to me negatively. Years had passed, and I ended up becoming a wizard, a certified sorcerer! Can you believe that God would use another sorcerer to deliver my dying soul from the pit of hell? This man told me I was introduced to demons by these people who had first introduced me to God. But I thought every church belong to God! Well I was so dead wrong. Here in Jamaica these churches are called revival and its members are known as revivalists. But the truth is they are all Satan's recruiters and these so-called churches are their recruiting centers. "For if he that cometh preacheth another Jesus, whom we have not preached, or if ye receive another spirit, which ye have not received, or another gospel, which ye have not accepted, ye might well bear with him (2 Corinthians 11:4)." These churches are run by Satan himself and the reason I can speak like this is because I was once one of his recruiting officers. Fifteen years had passed, and Satan owned me: mind, body and soul! I thought I was right with God, and then one day in 2004, Jesus Christ of Nazareth passed by and changed my life. I began to cry for my soul, "Lord, have mercy! Lord, have mercy!" Did you know that satanic worshippers can't call the Messiah, Jesus Christ of Nazareth? If they do, then the familiar spirits around them will have to leave and they will start to get spiritual deliverance. No unclean thing can go before the Father and stay in its dirty state! This is what God had taught me to keep (locked) me out of the spiritual realm of witchcraft. Yes, I can still do witchcraft if I so desire, but I choose to remain on God's side. Why? Because when I was on Lucifer's side, I was unable to see on God's side, however, when you are on God's side, you can see both *good and evil.*

Today, because of the knowledge and understanding that I have in Jesus Christ of Nazareth, I am best represented by the description offered in Geneses 3:22, "And the Lord God said, behold the man is become as one of us, to know good and evil: and now, lest he put forth his hand, and take also of the tree of life, and eat, and live forever;" God was the one who taught me how to keep myself out of the sorcery spiritual realm and witchcraft. He also taught me so now I offer this teaching to you the reader. Remember the following steps:

- Step one - learn to build a personal relationship with God!
- Step two - learn to renounce every spirit around you and in you, you acknowledge them, but you do not accept them. Hallelujah, unto God, in the name of Jesus Christ of Nazareth!

- Step three- rededicate your life and body back to Him as a reasonable sacrifice. "I beseech you therefore brethren, by the mercies of God, that you present your bodies a living sacrifice, holy, acceptable unto to God, which is your reasonable service (Romans 12:1)."

When I was saved about twenty years ago, I was still in captivity by a sex demon for years, yet I was professing that I was free! What made this worse is that I was still feeling the Holy Spirit every now and then. Remember, no unclean thing can go before the Father. Yes, we all have our weaknesses; they may come in different areas of our lives. The demon that held me in captivity was called "succubus" and had a form of masturbation. For hours each day I would play with myself until my flesh was satisfied sexually. The reason for this confession is to encourage you or any individual struggling with this demon, always encourage yourself! Doing this will help you to put it into subjection, exposing your weakness so that Satan will no longer have control over you. James encourages us to confess our sins one to another! Why? Because James 5:16 states, "Confess your faults one to another, and pray one for another, that ye may be healed. "The effectual fervent prayer of a righteous man availeth much."

You are going to make it! You are going to make it, I Did! I am a living witness and today I am giving God all the glory in the Name of Jesus Christ of Nazareth. "But if they cannot remain let them marry for it is better to marry than to burn (1 Corinthians

7:9)." Brothers and Sisters in Christ you will not lose your bad habits at one time when you first get baptized. It will take time, you are still at the processing plant and the refiner is still working on you. I hear you say in the spirit, "I have failed him again," "No! You didn't!" "Yes, you have fallen but now it is time for you to get back up and continue to walk with Him again." "What are you saying SpairLee? Are you encouraging someone to sin?" "Heavens No, but I am encouraging a fallen soldier to rise again and defend the name and honor of Jesus Christ of Nazareth."

The bible teaches that Jesus Christ of Nazareth saves and he keeps us, now if those wounded soldiers stayed down, Satan would laugh at us, and this would show that our savior had failed us. "Brethren, if a man be over taken in a fault, ye which are spiritual, restore such a one in the spirit of meekness; considering thyself, lest thou be tempted (Galatians 6:1)." When we fall under our cross, God is not surprised. The Bible said that Jesus Christ of Nazareth, while on his way to his death fell under his cross. This is to signify to you and I that sometimes we will falter but, we should get up again and continue our journey. Hebrews 4:15 tells us, "for we have not a high priest which cannot be touched, with the feeling of our infirmities; but was in all points tempted like as we are, yet without sin." Praise God, this prophecy was then fulfilled!

In 1991, I backslide! I was now sixteen years old, and my physical appearance was changing, and my body started to come alive. I got involved with a sister in the church I was attending. I found myself caught up in a love triangle. You see there were two young women at the time who let me know they were interested in me. Yes, I know you can identify with this! Who has not been young in church and had someone giving you the eye because you were anointed, or you were the preacher's son or daughter. Anyway, one evening I was on my way home, and one of the young women made her advance. I invited her to my home, my mother and sister were in the country at the time. We spent the whole evening talking and satisfying the flesh in ways that were only meant for marriage, not us! I was disobedient to the will of God, she was not my wife. The things we did that night should only be done between two people who have given themselves to God and committed themselves to each other for life in marriage. My young mate only wanted one thing from me. What a lesson for me to learn. The next day, she left for work. I received a call from the Pastor of the church. Would you believe that she told all her friends, including the other young women that we had sex! She told them I was good in bed and they could have me now because she got me first. I was disobedient to God! The way the situation was handled caused an up-roar in the church. I felt betrayed, cheap, used, and the worse of it all, I knew that I disobeyed God. These things caused me to leave the church and backslide.

Chapter Two

Exposing Demons of the Grave Realm

Message: Demons Are Real!

I was now exposed to the grave realm. There are two dimensions that Satan works from. Satan works the atmosphere, while his demons work from the grave realm. In the previous chapter, I was being exposed to the fallen angels. In this chapter it is the demons of the grave realm.

Did you know that there are four spirits that rule the earth?

1. The Spirit of God.
2. The spirit of Satan.
3. The spirit Man.
4. The spirit of Alcohol.

Question: Which one of these am I afraid of?

Answer: The spirit of man.

Question: Why am I afraid of the spirit of man?

Answer: We can reject the Spirit of God and He cannot force us to worship Him. Whenever God dwells on the inside, natural man is also present. We can rebuke Satan's spirit in the Name of Jesus Christ of Nazareth and believe yet, the spirit of man is also present within the body. We can simply refuse to drink Alcohol because we have the right to choose. But when the spirit of pride and self-righteousness consumes the heart of a man, he is a danger to himself and to others around him. Even though something or someone must rule over him, he can have all four spirits dwelling on the inside and they all can operate at once. The Spirit of God is the strongest of the spirits and He will always dominate the other spirits.

Now unto the Church of God.

Message: The Antichrist's spirit is here.

Did you know that Satan operates within a time frame? Witches and Wizards are more powerful and effective when they are casting spells around the hours of *6pm, 9pm, 12am and 3am.* Whenever any child of God is going to pray during these times, they will have to be *extremely careful and remember to separate the spiritual realms by using the name of Jesus Christ of Nazareth.* If not, the unsuspecting Christian will end up in a spiritual battle or worse end up becoming a Witch or Wizard.

Each evening, about 6pm, the Bishop of the church I was attending would have everyone gather around the altar to welcome the angels, who they believed were sent from God. The Bishop had many decorations on his altar: flowers, candles of all shapes, colors and sizes. Quart bottles filled with water believed to be for spiritual deliverances. There was a single white basin filled with water placed under the altar table, believed to offer protection from evil spirits.

This church was far more different from the one that I was coming from. In this church, we could be involved in any sexual relationship with anyone you like! As long as Bishop J knew about it, he would give you his blessings upon the relationship. At one-point allegations arose that one of the young ministers who was a police officer, was sleeping with the young girls inside our church. These are the attitudes and behaviors in the churches labeled the sixty-one (61) revivalists! But why? This was a means to keep us from becoming holy unto God. 1 Corinthians 3:16 "Know ye not that ye are the temple of God, and that the Spirit of God dwelled in you? 17 If any man defiles the temple of God, him shall God destroy; for the temple of God is holy, which temple ye are." These behaviors were not accepted by the sixty (60) revivalist groups where I came from. This was why Bishop J kept asking me questions I could not understand!! The Bishop would often ask me why was I there? Sometimes he would ask, "What did God tell you about me today?" On many occasions, I was then left wondering, "What the hell is he talking about." The duties of Bishop J were simply, he was preparing me for future priestly duties in the kingdom of darkness! I was already exposed to the highest realm in the kingdom of darkness, the Bishop wasn't sure what I was doing there, and I didn't know what he was talking about! The sixty revivalists group worshipped falling angels. Deep down inside they think that God is with them! Here I was being introduced to another spiritual realm by Bishop J. who had

19

his own church in St Ann. I later learned that this realm is known as the graveyard spirits!

The sixty-one (61) revivalists are easily identified. Why? They have to wear uniforms in order for the spiritual realm to open up unto them. They used the following items during their worship services: 1. Candles: which they used to represent, Jesus Christ of Nazareth: The light of the world. 2) Flowers: which were believed to charm or entertain the Holy Spirit. 3) Water: which was believed to represent, holiness unto our God, Purification, protection, deliverances, cutting spirits?

The sixty-one (61) revivalists wear material uniforms given to them by the spiritual realms or their leaders. Whenever they wear these uniforms, the spiritual realms are open to them and the familiar spirits are activated. How do I know this? I was a former high priest and a recruiting officer for Satan. I was exposed to the atmosphere demons, aka falling angels and the graveyard demons, aka ghosts or duppy! The graveyard realm is really an imitation of "Satan's holy ghost," Yes! Satan even tried to create or have his "own holy ghost." This was why the "Angel of God asked the question, "why does The Church seek the living God in the graveyard spirit realm?" Mark 16:6 And he saith unto them, be not affrighted: You seek Jesus Christ of Nazareth, which was crucified, he is risen, he is not here, behold the place where they laid him. These people refused to "wear the name of Jesus Christ of Nazareth as their true spiritual garment" instead they choose to wear color materials. Whenever you see someone in these colors, here is the true meaning:

1. Full khaki: This is believed to be one of the highest orders in spirit realm, why? This is said to be the "messenger angel Gabriel!" This is a lie from the pit of hell!

(2) Khaki and black: This is believed to be "Michael the angel of war." This is a lie from the pit of hell!

(3) Dark blue: This is believed to be "Miriam the healing angel." This is a lie from the pit of hell!

(4) The Bandana: This is believed to be the "angel Rachel." This is another lie and worse, not even biblical.

Satan has changed his strategy, he realized that the body of Jesus Christ of Nazareth is aware of these uniforms, so now only "his high priests are wearing the dress." Yes! "Those so-called preaching garments or Bishop's robes." These are only a version of the leaves that Adam and Eve sewde together to cover themselves! Satan's newest color is the color purple for robes. Why is this more "dangerous?" The meaning of the purple robe, is Satan's version of Jesus and Jesus Christ!" Yes! The Antichrist has now invaded our Church from the "highest level". Lately, I've seen Bishop's oversees in this purple dress. When I commented on it on social media, I was told that this was because the Bishop was on "special assignment in Africa," so he had to wear it. Garbage, I didn't even "make mine when I got it from the spiritual realm, why not? Real men don't "wear dresses!"

One Sunday morning, during worship service, the spirit realm opened, and all the people were dancing and shouting. It was then I saw a dirt pit for the first time in the midst of the church. It was a dirt hole about 24 inches in width with a depth about 6ft. Let me be clear, this was not a baptism pit, but one of a grave. One of the brothers jumped into the pit and they handed him a lighted candle to put inside. I am now ashamed of myself, that I once believed in such garbage; what madness! God gave them over to a reprobate mind to do those things which are not convenient (Romans 1:25-28). Let me state it categorically clear, these sorcerers or obeah-men don't believe that they are doing anything wrong, why not? 2 Corinthians 4:4 In whom the god of this world hath blinded the minds of them which believe not, lest the light of the glorious gospel of Christ, who is the image of God, should shine unto them. God only shares His secret with his friends. A Sorcerer or obeah-man can enter God's Holy Presence; therefore, no magician, sorcerer, or fortune teller can predict our future! God hates competitions, therefore he instructed us that we should not follow these wizards and witches who are claiming to foretell our future. Isaiah 42:8 I am the Lord: that is my name: and my glory will I not give to another, neither my praise to graven images.

Bishop J was very well known throughout Jamaica, people would come to him from all over the island: Our highest-ranking clients were "church people from all denominations." Then police officers were our second highest clients, the third were mostly men who were "murders" or brought up on gun related charges. They would each pay us a visit whenever they have a court date!! Bishop J would charge from $100,000 to $200,000, it is a very profitable business!

Bishop J was working with an assistant pastor, but when the assistant Pastor's wife filed for him to go to the United States the vacancy was now open and I was the best person to fill that position at the time. My duties were far different from Bishop J. I was working as a sorcerer or obeah-man but my duties also including me finding other upcoming sorcerers and recruit them and place them inside churches to "Pollute the Church from behind the pulpits." What?

> 2 Corinthians 11:4, 13-15 For if he that cometh
> preacheth another Jesus, whom have not preached
> or if you receive another spirit, which you have not
> received, or another gospel, which you have not
> acceptable, you might well bear with him. 13 For
> such are false apostles, deceitful workers,
> transforming themselves into the apostles of Christ.
> 14 And no marvel: for Satan himself is transformed
> into an angel of light. 15 Therefore it is no great
> thing if his ministers also be transformed as
> ministers of righteousness: whose end shall be
> according to their works.

My main duties were simply, to teach these potential gifted individuals how to use the *name of Jesus and Jesus Christ to open the spiritual realms.* If I visited a church and identified anyone, this was even be better and easier, why? They were already known by their church members, and they were already in familiar territories! Did I know what I was doing all those years before God cleansed me? No! God was the one who revealed all these things to me, after He was now able to trust me with His secret!!! My question to everyone reading this book is, "can God trust you?" Psalm 25:14 The secret of the Lord is with them that fear him: and He will show them His covenant.

One-week day, I was called by my Pastor to accompany him to the country. It was during this time in St. Thomas that I performed my first bath. You see, these spiritual rituals are often performed in Jamaica, to mimic or imitate the baptism of John the Baptism. The difference between the two is that here in Jamaica this particular bath, had no water immersion. This bath is performed while the individual is standing in a small room. What is the meaning of all this you may ask? This is a spiritual ritual to dedicate the person or persons into the spiritual realm. This spiritual ritual is also one of the ways in which we can open the door to the spirit realm negatively. The male or female would be physically washed (bathed) from head to toe, as they stood totally naked before the obeah man or spiritual high priest, while those in the congregation awaited their return. Those who were untutored in the spirit could have been turned on sexually by such an act. Yet, I stood there clothed in my everyday clothes, black pants and white shirt. I bathed the males first, then the females. One by one they came to have their sins removed by me.

The Bishop was by now preparing me for my new role at his side; it was believed that the spiritual realm had found favor with me. Weeks later, I was called to a private meeting with the bishop that taught me to work the grave spirit realm or an Obeah-man (sorcerer), in his room, funny. When I arrived in the room, immediately I could see the light of the television. The blue light on the screen let me know that he had just finished watching something or was about to. The Bishop began to speak in a low voice as he sat on the end of his bed. I was confused. "What the hell is going on here?" I kept asking myself. I was there staring at the bishop, he then turned his head towards the television; this man was now trying to direct my gaze toward the television to view whatever he was watching. Nothing was there but blue light and screen, then he pressed the remote control, now I was really "Confused." The bishop was now watching a XXX blue movie, he had already prepared the atmosphere for everything. I stood there in silence. What the hell is going on here, this wasn't a conversation, I was on a romantic date, the "Devil" is a liar from the pit of hell! *You see, he called this meeting to let me know that I was now at a point where I needed to choose how deep in the spirit realm I wanted to go or if I needed a higher level. Then he explained, for me to get higher spiritually, I had to sleep with him! Why? Sleeping with him would mean that I would have to be submissive unto him spiritually; this means that he would have* *total control over the spirits that would work within me!!!* "My God," I remember thinking at the time, "What the HELL was this man thinking?" You are a bishop, you preach the words of the Bible. Here in Jamaica it is heavily embedded in our culture to speak out against homosexuality, I was not even aware that the Bible spoke out against it. Imagine how I felt when I found, "For this cause God gave them up unto vile affections: for even their women did change the natural use into that which is against nature: 27 And likewise also the men, leaving the natural use of the woman, burned in their lust one toward another; men with men working that which is unseemly, and receiving in themselves that recompense of their error which was meet (Romans 1: 26-27)."

When this Bishop made the pass at me, I decided right then this was not of God. My love for God, kept me sane and free from acting out against this man. I felt so much anger; disappointment, and shame, that he would even think to ask such a thing of me. I immediately left his church and returned to Kingston. I found myself back at the church that I had left after being so humiliated from my prior sexual exploits. God would not let me go. My love for God and His word would not let me go; it kept pulling me back to God, like a moth drawn to a flame!

The Bishop was correct. I was ready to move deeper in the *spirit realm. You see, after returning to Kingston, I began to have* *more intense visions and open trances.* One night, I had a vision

26

that someone was asking me to feed my spirit. I didn't understand the vision, so I asked a woman in the community who was known for interpreting dreams and visions. After consulting with her I was told or instructed to buy two Red Strip Beers, now this is the official beer of Jamaica. I was told to punch a hole inside the unopened bottle and shake it up. Immediately after following her instructions, I felt a difference in my spirit. I tell you that night, I received yet another vision. This time the spirit was now thanking me for feeding them. You see unaware, I had opened one of the doors to the spiritual realm and as a reward for my obedience for feeding these spirits, I was now given my own demons to work within the spiritual realm, it was official, I was now a high priest of Lucifer, working against Jesus Christ of Nazareth.

A few weeks later, I found myself able to communicate with demonic spirits without being in a vision at night. The demons were now communicating with me openly as I began going in and out of trances more frequently. One Wednesday night during a praying and healing service, the spirits from the grave realm were present, now there was a spiritual warfare brewing in the atmosphere at the church. At that time I didn't know or understand what was going on, until I had gotten my total Spiritual cleansing and restoration. That night I was operating from both spiritual realms at the same time. The church that I was now worshipping in were the ones who taught me about the falling angels, my God. Being that I was now exposed to the grave realm spirits, I was now challenging them for spiritual power, and I wasn't even aware of this. For twenty-two years there was a constant spiritual battle going on inside of me, my God! I was now a walking battle ground, all three spirit realms were now inside of me fighting for total control, but God. Let me explain: 1) God's presence is always inside if we are alive physically, but it doesn't mean that he is in control. 2) Being that I was exposed to the falling angels, they too were now inside battling for control. 3) Now that I was given my own grave realm spirit, they too were defending themselves, while fighting for control. All three spiritual dimensions wanted total control; this is how I can explain what was going on inside of me, leading up to my total "Deliverance."

That night I was so caught up in the spirit realm, I can't even recall all that happened. The only thing I remember is having a glass of water thrown in my face and being told I couldn't come back to take over the church. It was no wonder that I left the church for twelve years, refusing to pray or call upon the name of Jesus, or Jesus Christ. I realized that doing so had me opening the grave realm, along with the spirits of falling angels. I can tell you now after reflecting on the situation, because I am totally delivered from demon possession. I realized that the Pastors and Bishops at that time were not able to offer me or anyone else deliverance because they too need to be delivered. They did not possess the key to deliverance! What is this key you ask? The name of Jesus Christ of Nazareth!

Chapter Three

Persecuted for Righteousness Sake

To God Be the Glory, In the Name of Jesus Christ of

Nazareth: Now unto the Churches

Message: How Far Would You Go to Destroy Someone?

Long before I met my wife I was living with Joy B. We spent about eighteen months together and I had to end the relationship simply because she brought the worst out of me. When you are in a relationship, it must spark growth! If you are not a better person in that relationship, better than what you were before you entered it, then a re-evaluation of your place in that relationship should be done quickly! You see, Joy B. tried to beat the hell out of me and I almost killed her in my house while defending myself against her attacks. I was on my way to work one morning when I saw Sister Jackie L. and Joy B. conversing with each other. This was nothing new, they always talked, and I passed them without saying a word to any of them. When I came from work that day, I had to run two young converts from my home. My wife was new to the community and the two young converts were her only friends. I later apologized to my wife and encourage her to seek older friends. I told her that these were children, they are light headed, young minded. That night we were told by one of the young convert sister Tonie, that the church members were jealous of the

29

relationship with my wife. My wife and I were the only married couple who sat together in their church, and they hated it, but why? Bishop L. and his wife were always arguing with each other, was this the same behavior they expected from us? Few weeks later, allegations surface that I was sexually involved with sister Tonie; this was running ramped among the congregation. These rumors were started by Joy B and Sister Jackie L., Yes, the Bishop's wife! But why? Joy B was angry with me for leaving her and marrying someone else, while Sister Jackie L was angry with her husband the bishop for ordaining me a Deacon of their family business (church).

I asked Bishop L if he was aware of the rumors, naturally he claimed that he didn't know anything about these alleged allegations, which was started by his wife. He told me to let him handle it, because he was the Bishop, I agreed I would let him handle it. He wanted to handle it privately too, "to HELL with that!" I felt myself getting angry and feeling misunderstood. I was loud, shouting and getting ticked off the more I stood there thinking, then I told him, "this is my integrity we are talking about. Let the church judge this matter openly." The Bible says in Matthew 18:15, "Moreover if your brother shall trespass against thee, go and tell him his fault between thee and him alone. If he shall hear thee, though hast gained thy brother. You see, it was the Bishop and his wife who were openly judging me. I was not ready to defend myself openly and they knew it! Don't you understand that demons know your weaknesses? I called Sister Tonie to try and resolve the matter. It was then after not being able to reach her, I had a rather frank conversation with her mother. I asked her mother if she knew anything about these rumors, it was then I learned that the Bishop's wife started these rumors.

You see, the Bishop's wife, believed that I should not be given the position of a Deacon. She believed it was a family business and the next in line should be her son and her daughter. She wanted the church to be for the family. She feared that if I would be given the position of Deacon, this would topple her well-founded house of faith! Yes, I agree, stupid! She was the Bishop's wife! The issue was that she felt because she was in the church for about thirty-two years, she deserved the right to have a higher position, like that of, "Pastor!" What she didn't realize or understand is that her husband was the Bishop. All blessings flow from the head down! Had she just remained patient and committed to will of God, seeking the righteousness of the kingdom, all things would have been given to her in due time. The Bible tells us in Matthew 6:33, "But seek ye first the kingdom of God and all His righteousness; and all these things will be added unto you."

I couldn't wait to hang the phone up! "Hypocrites," I shouted at everyone inside the church and I was loud about it! I didn't care who heard me, I later found out we had visitors that day, two female friends who were also there to give them spiritual support. These women were a part of a wicked deceitful plot to come against me and have others to witness the humiliation and defeat. They received a lesson that day on just how far people would go to destroy another, even inside the church. How could someone be so evil, can you imagine! I was now their ordained Deacon by Bishop L, this was very significant because I was the first ever to be ordained in this church. One-night God visited me in a vision and told me that it was not my time yet to reign: I was not fully delivered from the spirit of witchcraft, neither was I spiritually matured. The Bishop's wife was not pleased with the ordination; she and about seven other Elders of the church began a fast that lasted seven days. When she called for the congregation to fast, I declined to join the fasting, spiritually the church wasn't doing well, so I thought that the fasting was for the growth of the church, but it was to stop me from being ordained as their Deacon and to keep me silent from proclaiming the name of Jesus of Jesus Christ of Nazareth, let me explain?

They told the bishop that I was operating in the spirit of witchcraft, and this seven days fasting was supposed to close the spiritual realms around me. The bishop accepted their challenge, but when the seven days fasting was over, my God: I felt the power of the Holy Spirit, and I began to shout, it was after church, I learned about the challenge, isn't God awesome? The Bishop's wife was now leading a rebellious team against her own husband, after knowing his plans for me. A minister from the church confirmed that the Bishop's wife really was plotting to over throw her own husband. This plot ran deeper than the church; it was even manifested in her home as she withheld intimacy from her husband. The minister from the church came to visit at my home one evening; I realized that he was on his phone with someone while talking to my wife and me. He was now having a dual conversation that was not going very well. The minister was there to offer me a deal with the devil, on the behalf of the bishop wife. He wanted to make a deal with me to keep silent about what I was receiving from the spirit realm. You see, the Bishop gave me the authority to come directly to him whenever I received a revelation or word from God. Yes, I was the Bishop's spiritual advisor of sorts, and the Ministers and Evangelist were not comfortable with this. See, the job of the Deacon is to protect the Bishop, so they thought. 1Timothy 3:1-2, 12 tells us clearly that, "This is a true saying, if a man desires the office of the Bishop he desires a good work. 2 A Bishop must be blameless, the husband of one wife, given to hospitality. 12 Let the Deacons be the husband of one wife, ruling their children and their own houses well. For they that have used the office of a deacon well purchase to themselves a good degree, and great boldness in the faith which is in Christ Jesus." So, the minister came to offer me a deal! He kept asking me to repeat what was being said clearly as if the other person was listening. I asked, "Who is on the phone minister?" "It's one of my daughters," he replied. As the conversation went on, she began calling the Bishop names and disrespecting him. My wife and I were floored. We were silent because we didn't know who was on the other end of that line.

About two weeks later, after Sabbath class, I was called to the Bishop's office at the church, during that meeting; a complete disclosure of the plot against the Bishop was disclosed. The master mind, his own wife! His wife wanted the leadership of the church. I was the one they feared so, the minister was sent to recruit me. It was revealed that the Bishop's wife had spent thirty-two years of her life in the church with her husband; she felt there was nothing to show for it. She was jealous of her husband's anointing and role as the shepherd. A jealous wife's deception! When they realized that I would not be a part of the plot, The Bishop's wife decided to force me out of the business (church), she gave her husband an ultimatum that if he didn't " Retract my Ordination" she was going to leave their marital home. It was then the Bishop told me that I was no longer their Deacon, my God: aren't you glad that God didn't allow "Mankind to select souls for Heaven"?

One of the sisters from the church gave me a message one day, according to her Bishop B wanted to see me, who is Bishop B? Bishop B is the same person who taught me the falling angels' spiritual realm. The Devil is a liar! You see, this was a plot to have me leaving their family business (church). Remember previously we spoke regarding the church that I was kicked out of, well, twelve years later that unfinished business returned to me. The bishop wife is the sister of my childhood sweetheart who was now approaching 50 and unmarried. When I turned back to the church, they thought that I was going to settle down and marry her. We would become the newest Deacon and Deaconess. I would then be excepted and welcomed into their family business (church). Yes, she seemed to forget the fact that I was already married! No, she didn't. She wanted me completely out the picture as she too was jealous because I married another.

A jealous wife's deception! When I refused to leave their family business (church), they decided to take matter into their own hands. One Saturday morning, I was inside my bathroom about to get ready for Sabbath class. It was then that I heard the Bishop outside with his sister in law, yes, the same one who was my childhood sweetheart, they were speaking with a well-known community leader. The Bishop was my spiritual leader, the shock and pain I felt when I realized he was seeking the aid from an alleged gunman to have me physically removed from his families place of business (church). He told the gunman that I was intimidating members of his church and I was not from the area. The gunman was the leader of a well-known gang in the Kingston area at the time. "A gun-shot the boy should get!" This was the judgment Bishop laid out for me while my church Elders were standing there. Why didn't they just ask me to leave their church? When I arrived at the church, Sabbath class had already begun. I wait for the opening session where anyone could ask questions. I was hurt and very angry, so I stood and began to ask my question.

35

"Should anyone in a church, seek the aid of a gunman to get rid of a member?" The Bishop glared at me as he told me to take my wife and leave. You see, he was upset with me because of my actions a few weeks ago. He wanted to handle the sex allegations against me; but in private! While they were already trying it openly, hypocrites!

I waited until the following Monday morning, when I saw the so-called community leader. He was already judging a young man who was badly beaten by members of his gang almost killed. Now the young man mother, being hurt by the beating of her son, was now begging the gunman to let him stay in the community because he had nowhere else to go. The gunman/community leader was now the judge and jury of his case. He and only he would decide if this young man would live and continue to reside in the community. The young man was told that the only way he could stay, if he took his beating, and don't get the police involved, only then can he remain in the community. Yes, gangs are everywhere, even in the streets of Jamaica! The case of the young man was now complete and closed, now my case was open. "Have I ever disrespected you?" I asked. "No," he replied. "Then how dear you pass judgment on me? I was in my bathroom Saturday, when I heard you telling the Bishop that a gunshot is what I should get." When I look back on the situation now, I couldn't blame the gunman; he thought that he was doing a favor for God. Even if he was satisfying his own selfish desires of recognition, control, and power. He didn't think anyone was brave enough to talk to him the way I had.

I was on my way from work few days earlier, when God revealed to me that this man was going to be killed. I began to pray and ask God for mercies on his behalf, mercies were granted, this man had another opportunity to repent, but didn't. I knew that once they took this young man out, at that time, it was a matter of time the powers that be would come after me. This young man had a Godly heart, on many occasions; members of his gang would seek to beat and threaten to kill me the ex-sorcerer. According to the allegations, I was the one working "witchcraft on the people in the community" WOW, the revelation of God came to pass; as gunmen invaded the community one night, and a shootout, "I was told" took place. It was also believed that it was a contract killing and the gunman/community leader was now their target! I reminded him, "they were coming to kill you a few days ago, do you remember that? They would have succeeded had I not interceded on your behalf when God revealed it to me and yet you stand here passing judgment on me?" "Aren't you afraid of God?" I asked! While pointing to the bullets holes in the walls I said, "Touch me and those gunshots holes won't be in the wall next time, but inside of you. You must always be careful of the things you speak against a man of God: God was the one who send me with a message to the church; they refused to take corrections from God. That is why they are getting you involved." Few years later,

Inspired by God

I heard that the gunman/community leader had been shot in the head! Four years he had to repent, he chose to walk in disobedience. How do I know? I told the young man that God would restore his marriage and family, God's words came to pass, but he did not heed the warning, when I told him not to return to his old ways. He is dead now, only because of his disobedience unto the voice of God!

Chapter Four

For the Prophets

To God be the Glory, In the Name of Jesus Christ of Nazareth:
Now unto the Young Prophets & Prophetess
Message: Don't be Afraid of Their Titles and Faces.

"Have not I commanded thee? Be strong and of a good Courage; be not afraid, neither be thou dismayed; for the Lord thy God is with thee whithersoever thou goest (Joshua 1:9)."

On Sunday March 26, 2017, I was physically thrown out of a church in Portmore Saint Catherine by a well-known pastor of the gospel. After learning about this pastor during an interview on Love 101 Radio Station, I decided to visit him the following Sunday. This pastor came highly recommended by one of the pastors during the interview. When I visited his church that first Sunday morning Wow, he was far below my expectations. Spiritually this Pastor wasn't even a spiritual baby he is one of the blindest church leaders I have met so far. During the worship service God revealed to me that he was not in total control over the church. This pastor called me up during the service and said, "Spair Lee I am not afraid of you." I thought to myself, how stupid can this man be, even if he thought that I was spiritually possess with demons ... this is not the way that God teaches us to do spiritual warfare or Spiritual deliverances. "For the weapons of our

39

warfare are not carnal, but mighty through God to the pulling down of strong-holds (2 Cor 10:4)" personally if I were still a sorcerer, this would be the easiest spiritual battle ground, and victory! Why? 1) I would have used the spirits of pride against him, along with his ignorance towards the spiritual realms, he didn't know them.

After church I was invited into the Pastors office while inside his office, he introduced me to two of his spiritual armor bearers (body guards). Wow! One was a sorcerer, still on Lucifer side, and the other one was either spiritually dead or spiritually sleeping. I told the three of them what God had revealed to me while still sitting in their presence. I waited until the two men left the office, then I turned to the Pastor and told him, "if I was still a sorcerer; I would have used his own two spiritual armor bearer (body guards) against him." I spoke directly with the sorcerer and explained to him that for him to be delivered, he needed to pray, fast, and renounce the evil spirits around him in the Name of Jesus Christ of Nazareth!

Young Prophets and Prophetesses please, I beseech you in the name of Jesus Christ of Nazareth, do not let these self-proclaimed spiritual leader's titles fool you! The only spiritual leader you and I have is the "Holy Spirit of the living God." "But the Comforter, which is the Holy Ghost, whom the Father will send in my name, he will teach you all things, and bring all things to your remembrance, whatsoever I have said unto you (John 14:26)" From to the beginning of time, we were taught by our parent that

Should Women Be Allowed to Preach and Teach the Gospel? Satan is always trying to destroy us, but have you ever stopped to consider why? While I was sitting in my bedroom on my bed, I began to wonder why is it that Satan hates you and me so much. With all these questions and signs kept popping up, I decided to consult the best person who can answer all these questions, Yes God! When I open (God) the bible, instantly the Holy Spirit ministers to my spirit, revealing just why Satan hates you and I so much.

1. First, Satan's issue is not with us but against God: The fact that we all bear the breath of God inside our body, we automatically become Satan's enemies.

2. Second, When Satan rebelled and sinned against God: the bible tells us that God immediately put Satan in chains until the Day of Judgment. Satan was bound for judgment but why? "And the angels which kept not their first estate, but left their own habitation, he hath reserved in everlasting chains under darkness unto judgment of the great day (Jude 1:6)."

3. Third, When Adam and Eve rebelled and sinned against God, why didn't they get the same punishment? They did not get the same punishment because at the time of their sins, they were still innocent of "Evil", knowing God: he never charged someone for what they don't know, or without first warning them.

41

4. Fourth, Satan thought that after we sinned against God: everything would have ended there between God and us, but he was so wrong.

5. Fifth, God stood up in our defense, and immediately, prepared a way to redeem us back unto Himself. My question is, "was God fair in His judgment concerning Satan?" Now God never judge His creations before first warning them, it is just in God's nature to do Righteousness! Satan "Must had known good and evil from the beginning for God to judge him" but he still went ahead and "Choose" to sin against God. Adam and Eve only knew good and evil after they sinned. "And the Lord God said, Behold, the man is become as one of us, to know good and evil; and now, lest he put forth his hand, and take also of the tree of life, and eat, and live forever (Genesis 3:22)." Let me explain this verse Spiritually: After mankind choose to sin against God, immediately God's government was called together, explaining that mankind chooses to become gods, they choose to rejected Heaven government and have their own, and now I "God decided by Myself" to put them out of my presence, before they also "choose" to use the knowledge of the tree of immortality wrongly too and become immortal while living inside the body of sins, flesh has to die. Yes! It was always in God's plan for mankind to live and reign on the earth in His presence forever; we were

created to be immortal beings living in God's government, but when mankind "choose" to rebel against God, we became "immortally dead." God immediately choose to redeem us back unto Himself, by taking on the form of a man. Yes! Jesus Christ of Nazareth. "And the Word was made flesh, and dwelt among us, (and we beheld his glory, the glory as of the only begotten of the Father) full of grace and truth (John 1:14)." Why? Colossians 2:9-10 For in him dwelleth all the fullness of the Godhead body. And you are complete in him, which is the head of all principality and power. The Godhead immediately chooses to restore humanity back to their rightful place after they sinned, whenever we repent and accept Jesus Christ of Nazareth as our personal savior! We are now given back dominion over Satan and all his demonic forces, yes! This was God's original plan from the beginning, when he placed Satan on earth, Adam and Eve's and all their offspring were ordained to rule over Satan. To God be all the glory in the name of Jesus Christ of Nazareth: Now we have the right not only to pass down judgment but also blessings from one generation unto the next, through the mighty name of Jesus Christ of Nazareth.

6. (Six) What makes the hatred even worst? This amazing Grace is infallible, it cannot be repossessed, it cannot be bought or sold, it is just unstoppable, saving from

generation to generations, but the best part of this all, what? It is "Impartial and Free" thank you God, in the mighty name of Jesus Christ of Nazareth!

It is important for you to understand as you read this, that when Adam and Eve sinned against God, the human race began to fail at that very moment. Genesis 2:5 God tells Adam, "I will put enmity between you and the woman and between your descendants and her Descendant. He will crush your head, and you will bruise His Heel." God having all wisdom and understanding knew that He had to do something, by taking on the identity of mankind: which was an honor for man; but insult to Satan.

7. The seventh important concept to consider is this, John 3:16 tells us, "God gave his only begotten son, that whosoever believeth in him would not perish but have everlasting life"

I have always believed that this was not possible; for us to live a holy life into God while living in the flesh. But I've come to realize that this was a lie from Satan. Anything that God expected of us is possible. Matthew 5:48 Be you therefore perfect, even as your Father which is in heaven is perfect. All of us can live a holy life unto God; it is a matter of our choices and the determination to change our bad habits. God requires Holiness from each one of us, in fact the Bible teaches, that without Holiness, none of us will ever see God! Leviticus 11:44 states, "I am the Lord thy God; ye

Should Women Be Allowed to Preach and Teach the Gospel? shall therefore sanctify yourselves, and ye shall; be holy; for I am holy; neither shall ye defile yourselves with any manner of creeping things that creepeth upon the earth." 1 Peter 1:9 reiterates this, "Because it is written, Be ye holy for I am holy." God requires this of every one of His children. It is one of the prerequisites of dwelling with Him in heaven. If God requires it, then it can be done!

When we ponder questions like these, it is important to go back to the beginning to find these answers. You see, the book of Genesis taught us that God is holy and all powerful; He is our creator, father, provider, sustainer, and friend. The best part of all of this is that, we share the same breath of our Holy God. He breathed the breath of life into each of us, whenever we repent and accept Jesus Christ of Nazareth as our personal savior! Therefore, I am instantly Holy! The task for us then, is to remain in this state of Holiness, especially when we consider we were all born in sin and shaped in iniquity. Genesis 2:7 tells us, "And the Lord God formed man of the dust of the ground and breathed into his nostrils the breath of life; and man became a living soul. When we fall out of the will of God we become like the first Adam, dead, just laying still, wasting our lives away until God, through Jesus Christ of Nazareth breathes new life back into us. I can't speak for you but, my body was stinking rotten, all hope was lost, until I finally heard the shout, that Jesus Christ of Nazareth was passing by. I had to find a way for my soul to be restored!

45

But can this be so? Yes, He left heaven, came to earth, bled, suffered and died for you and me, so that we might have the right to life and life more abundantly. Jesus Christ of Nazareth came just for me, just for you, to restore us back to the Father. It is because of this I now understand the words of Jesus Christ of Nazareth as recorded by John in John 11:25, "I am the resurrection, and life; he that believeth in me, though he were dead, yet shall he live."

A Holy God, plus my messed-up situations, equaled mercy, love and forgiveness. When I consider that Jesus Christ of Nazareth, left his place in glory, took on the nature of man, just to offer me a second chance; giving me a first-class ticket to heaven, I can't help but to scream Hallelujah! "Thank You God, for loving me." But wait, the offer does not stop with that first class ticket to heaven, I am now offered an inheritance. I am a son of God! "Hallelujah!" Wait, there's more, 1 Peter 2:9, tells us, we are a "chosen generation, royal priesthood, a holy nation." You must begin to Praise God for this! I'll give you a few seconds to get your Praise on! One…. two...three…Hallelujah!

See, I told you we can be holy unto God if we choose to be! It's all about the choices we make. Let him forsake evil and do good: for the eyes of the Lord are over the righteous, and his ears, open to their prayers (1Peter 3:11-12). I surrendered and experienced this, 1 John 3:9, tells us, "Whosoever is born of God doth not commit sin; for his seed remaineth in him; and cannot sin, because he is born of God." Many Christians over the years have

46

Should Women Be Allowed to Preach and Teach the Gospel? always dreamed of becoming or desired to be demon slayers. Everyone wants to pray and demonstrate how powerful they are in the spirit realm but, be mindful that the first and worst demons we should battle or even bind up is "Self." This demon called, "SELF" will stop you from rebuking all other demons and will cause the children of God to become ineffective or worse, (LUKE WARM). 2 Corinthians 10:5 tells us that, "Casting down imaginations, and every high thing, that exalteth itself, against the knowledge of God and bringing into captivity every thought to the obedience of Christ." Christian's can't be effective until this demon is put under spiritual subjection! Disobedience and rebellion against God, will plunge even the best of us into the spirit of witchcraft. 1 Samuel 15:22-23, tells us, "And Samuel said, hath the Lord as great delight in burnt offering and sacrifices, as in obeying the voice of the Lord? Behold, to obey is better than sacrifice, and to hearken than the fat of rams. For rebellion is as the sin of witchcraft, and stubbornness is as iniquity and idolatry. Because thou hast rejected the word of the Lord, He hath also rejected thee from being king."

On May 7, 2013, I met a Pastor who was the earthly shepherd of an Apostolic Church in Kingston. Spiritually he was doing well, with a very powerful ministry for God. Did you know Pastors can easily lose their way too? Many powerful men and women over the years throughout the Bible have strayed away from God, because of the poor choices or bad decisions they made! Consider

47

Gehazi the servant of Elisha; this man of God was next in line to receive the favor and blessing of Almighty God.

> "But Gehazi the servant of Elisha the man of God said, behold my master hath spared Naaman this Syrian, in not receiving at his hands that which he brought: but, as the LORD liveth, I will run after him and take somewhat of him. 21 So Gehazi followed after Naaman. And when Naaman saw him running after him, he lighted down from the chariot to meet him, and said, is all well? 22 And he said, all is well, my master hath sent me, saying, Behold, even now there become to me from mount Ephraim two young men of the sons of the prophets: give them I pray thee, a talent of silver, and two changes of garments (2 Kings 5:20-22)."

The Pastor was doing fine. He was on his way to receiving the perfect will of God, until he received a "priestly" materialistic robe from a false prophet. You see, the Pastor lost his way immediately. He is now living in the permissive will of God instead of the complete perfect will of God. Why? The monetary gifts promised in exchange for his soul by that false prophet. The false prophet died a few weeks after recruiting the Pastor and a few from his congregation. God never leaves anything undone! This should have raised the suspicions of the pastor as to why he was given that materialistic robe. There is still hope for this Pastor, still room for him to repent and change before the breath leaves his nostril. I will be praying for him and his congregation! Romans 3 tells us, "For all have sinned, and come short of the glory of God." When I think of all the years I constantly failed God, He had every right to discard me and throw me into the rejected pile. Notice: I said (the) reject pile and not (His) reject pile, why not? Simple, God does not have a rejected pile! God does not make junk, but I will hastily say, I embodied all things rejected. I was like this until God, rejuvenated (made me young) again.

It all began when I was about fourteen years old. I was full of zeal for God but, everything was not perfect. No matter what was going on, I wouldn't let go or give up on God. No wonder God called us children and not adults. When I reach the age of eighteen years old, I had a total different view about God. Why? I had begun to think like the adults, (wolves in sheeps clothing), no disrespect to anyone. By now we all should understand why God called us children and not adults. Why? Simple, children though they may not like it at first or comply willing, do obey rules. Adults on the other hand, tend to make excuses and whine their way out of things. Well, I was guilty of trying to do just that, God said one thing, but I ended up, doing my own thing. Any time "self" checks in, God checks out. Why? Revelation 3:20 tells us, "Behold, I stand at the door and knock; sif any man hear my voice, and opens the door, I will come in to him, and will sup with him, and he with me."

After I left church, I began to think about how funny we adults (backsliders) are. We always seem to cast the blame on everyone else for our failed relationships. Have you ever wondered why we never blame ourselves. Why? That is the nature of adults, when

(Satan) thought that he was now old enough to fend or provide for himself, he thought that he didn't need God anymore. Did you know that even "Satan" needs God to survive? As soon as I began to see himself as an adult, that's when all hell broke loose upon my life. Did you know that Satan is not an original adult, but a look alike adult? I hear you saying, "what do you mean?" Well, I 'll tell you! Original adults can take care of themselves and their children or love ones. God is the perfect example of who and what an adult should be. He made all the provisions for himself and all His children who depend on him.

God is such a loving Father and a great provider that He even provided a home for Lucifer! Why? Lucifer was unable to provide for himself after being evicted from heaven. Satan's new home is where? Matthew 25:41 tells us, "Then shall he say also unto them on the left hand, depart from me, ye cursed into everlasting fire, prepared for the devil and his angels." Is there any doubt that God truly loves you? Well let me help you settle that doubt, I was an enemy of God, a former sorcerer, I should be dead without repentance. But, God gave me a second chance through the blood of Jesus Christ of Nazareth. Today! I must first thank God as He has blessed me with his Holy Spirit, and the gift of discernment of Spirits. I am also thanking Him, for entrusting me with the responsibilities of identifying His Fallen Prophets and Prophetesses, while giving me the knowledge to restored them back to their former glory, in the name of Jesus Christ of Nazareth.

Should Women Be Allowed to Preach and Teach the Gospel? Over the past few years, I have encountered some of the finest soldiers of God. Now I will not call any names, but know this, if I started, I wouldn't have enough pages inside this book to list them all! I have had the honor of meeting so many Elders, Evangelists, Pastors, Missionaries, Prophets Prophetesses and Teachers of the gospel of Jesus Christ of Nazareth. Yes, I have encountered the five-fold ministry quite often.

I've often shared that God was the one who called and ordained, not me. You see, as God calls and ordains, He sends His blessings to accompany you, for the work of the kingdom. God has equipped His people with mega churches. Yes! "Facebook, Twitter, Periscope, U-tube, etc.," to preach and teach his unadulterated word. All of this He gave so that His gospel would be preached and the lost souls of this world would hear and return to their first love.

Social media today can be one of the largest means of reaching the masses, if used properly. My brothers and sisters, I employ you to use your time in the pulpit wisely. Some of you (us) wouldn't have the option of speaking in a church ran by man! Because He truly knows what's best for us, God had a master plan already in place. God wants me to remind you, never be discouraged and never lose faith. God says, "I God am with you always even unto the end." Joshua 1:9 tells us, "Have not I commanded thee? Be strong and of a good courage; be not afraid, neither be thou dismayed; for the Lord thy God is with thee

51

whithersoever thou goest." I know that God cannot lie or go back on his words, neither can he change his mind. He just cannot do that, it is just not in His nature. If God promised it, then we have nothing to fear, in the name of Jesus Christ of Nazareth.

I beseech you, in the name of Jesus Christ of Nazareth, let us therefore stop comparing ourselves to the (place of worship) and use whatever means available to preach the gospel. In fact. Why not use your (Facebook) account, or any other social media as your pulpit, (platform) to minister to God's people. We are officially out of time, yet there is still work to do. Matthew 28:19-20, tells us, "Go ye therefore, and teach all nations, baptizing them in the name of the Father, and of the Son, and of the Holy Ghost. Teaching them observe all things what-so-ever I have commanded you: and, lo, I am with you always, even unto the end of the world."

Over the years, many Christians and Christians at heart have long desired to become spiritually mature. Sometimes they would fast and pray for hours, sometime even days, without getting their deliverance or worse, not hearing from God. How could this happen? God has taught me over the years that He is not impressed with our sacrifices, fasting, long prayers, but with our Obedience unto Him! 1 Samuel 15:22 tells us, "Behold to obey is better than sacrifices, *and* to hearken than the of ram's fats." Many Christians today, would rather spend days in fasting and long prayers, when all they needed are these five fruits of the spirits to grow and spiritually mature. These fruits are as following:

52

1. **Love:** Thou shalt love the Lord thy God and thy neighbor as thyself, on these two commandments hangs all the law. Matthew 22:37-40 tells us, "Jesus said unto him, thou shall love the Lord thy God with all thy heart, and with all thy soul, and with all thy might. This is the first and greatest commandment. And the second is like unto it, thou shalt love thy neighbor as thyself."

2. **Obedience:** 1 Samuel 15:22 tells us "And Samuel; said, Hath the Lord as great delight in burnt offerings and sacrifices, as in obeying the voice of the Lords? Behold, to obey is better than sacrifice, and to hearken than the fat of rams."

3. **Repentance**: Romans 3:23 tells us, "For all have sinned and come short of the glory of God."

4. **Forgiveness:** Luke 4:22 tells us, "And all bare him witness, and wondered at the gracious words which proceeded out of his mouth. And they said, is not this Joseph's son"

5. **Praises**: Psalms 100:1 tells us, "Make a joyful noise unto the Lord, all ye lands, serve the Lord with gladness; come before his presence with singing.

Statement: King David was able to have a very personal relationship with God; he was able to touch God, even at the lowest point in his life. Why? David had learned his rights of the Spiritual realm and began to live according to these principles, this

53

automatically brought God's attention. You see, when these principles are observed, the worshippers force God to open heaven, listen to their cries, and supply their needs!

Philippians 4:19, tells us, "But my God shall supply all your need according to his riches in glory by Christ Jesus." What does this mean? God is an awesome Father and he loves all His children. He is waiting on them to accept His presence and government through Jesus Christ of Nazareth. All our daily supplies shall be released immediately from His heavenly government to us, His People. God is only a rewarder, let me explain? Galatians 6:7 tells us, "Be not deceived; God is not mocked: for whatsoever a man soweth, that shall he also reap." The true meaning of the verse: *Please don't bring any folly in my presence, period. I am God, you cannot fool me because I know your thoughts, even before they happen. If you do badly I know, if you do good, I know, because I am a judge who renders righteous judgements. You will get exactly what you deserve, good or bad. The choice is up to you, so choose wisely.*

Many Christians spend time fasting and praying, seeking to become Spiritual, rather than have a personal relationship with God! They seek after signs and miracles, why? The flesh always seeks attention, craves power, and recognition in this world. While this is normal and acceptable to the world, this is a problem with God. Why? God does not like competitions, and worse Yes! Worse, God does not share His glory with anyone else or anything.

Should Women Be Allowed to Preach and Teach the Gospel? After years of walking in God's presence, I've come to understand that the worse sin we can commit is putting ourselves or something else before God.

We must begin to change our selfish mindset. Instead of seeking to become more spiritual, more time should be spent seeking a closer relationship with God! To become spiritual, it requires that we study the word of God daily, why? Only the word of God is qualified to test and try the spirits in the spirit realm. Lucifer operates from the spirit realm. You see, Lucifer's frequency intersects with the minds of men and distorts messages intended for their good. For example, have you ever heard a radio station playing two messages at the same time? Well this is exactly what can and does happen to us. When it does happened, understand that it is only the word of God that will rightly fine tune the frequency of man back to His frequency.

2 Timothy 2:15 tells us, "Study to shew thyself approved unto God, a workman that needeth not to be ashamed, rightly dividing the word of truth." What is the true meaning of this verse? *You must learn the word of God for yourself! When temptations come, and they will, you will stand upon the word of God. You will use that word to rebuke the whiles of the enemy. The key to slaying the enemy is using the mighty name of Jesus Christ of Nazareth. If you do not begin to utilize this key, you will be defeated and become ashamed, disqualifying yourself from the inheritance offered.*

55

Inspired by God

The word of God is the only defense. God's word is God Himself! The word started with Him and it will finish with Him! God through His words rules and governs the spiritual realm. He is a resource all by Himself in the spirit realm! He depends on nothing to operate or to survive in the spirit realm, period!

The reason why we have so many sorcerers today, is simply because they don't know God personally, they were busier seeking after signs and wonders, rather than seeking God. These demonic spirits are parasites, believe me, they are not able to live on their own; they need God, in order for them to move or act. All life form depends upon God, this includes Satan, he needs God! For you and me to operate or survive in the spirit realm and remain clean: we need to have a personal relationship with God: and a great temple to worship. But today, Satan as recruited his own Ministers, then categorically place them inside our temples, this is why we have so many fake churches and fake people who call themselves Christians. But wait, God is forced again, to defend himself. Why? God must do everything to remain blameless. He defends himself with what actions. Galatians 6:7 tells us, "Be not deceived, God is not mocked; for whatsoever a man soweth, that shall he also reap. "God was forced to take this action to protect the body of Jesus Christ of Nazareth. We are the body of Christ, we must desire to have a clean heart so that we can do His will. We must present ourselves "Spiritually clean before God." 1 Peter 4:17 tells us, "For the time is come that judgment must begin at the house of God,

Should Women Be Allowed to Preach and Teach the Gospel? and it first begins at us, what shall the end be of them that obey not the gospel of God? And if the righteous scarcely be saved, where shall the sinners appear?" The meaning of this verse:

Now tell me, if those people who attend church every Sunday find it hard with God, when they don't surrender totally unto Jesus Christ of Nazareth as Lord and savior, then what am I, a sinner to do? How will I survive before His wrath to come? Seeing that I have rejected His presence and calling on so many occasions.

Statement: I was one such person, rather than seeking to know God personally, I got caught up in spiritual signs and miracles. This was how I opened the door to the spirit realm. Satan began to reveal himself to me in dreams, showing me all sorts of things to use to heal people, another lie from the pit of Hell. Remember this, my beloved brothers and sisters in Jesus Christ of Nazareth, only the name of Jesus Christ of Nazareth can defend us against the enemy or heal our disease. Yes! Nothing but the name of Jesus Christ of Nazareth, nothing or no one else. **Question:** Spair Lee am I to believe that all the other people who only called him Jesus or Jesus Christ are not spiritually cleansed and they are all sorcerers?

Answer: Heavens NO! This only applies to all those that Satan tampered with. For example, let's say an expected mother, "our church having a crusade seeking soul" and the hospital "church ground" was not dedicated to God properly, then the delivery theater "Altar area is not cleaned. Whenever a baby or babies are born "new converts start repenting" and accepted Jesus Christ, because the church ground was not dedicated properly, chances are those "new converts" will become spiritually infected with a disease, (familiar spirits). Now if the midwives "altar workers" or doctors (Bishop's and Pastors) don't know how to handle this delicate situation. Then all those babies with the disease "converts with the familiar spirits" will become spiritually handicap and end up being "wizards or witches".

Question: If this happens what can be done to correct it?

Answer: The babies, (converts) are already born spiritual handicaps, (sorcerers) nothing can be done to change that, however; these babies will now need special attention whenever you are ready to "teaching them" how to talk, instead of saying, "Jesus or Jesus Christ" you will now have to say (Jesus Christ of Nazareth)! Did you catch that? If not, you and your entire church will plunge into the spirit of witchcraft!

Question: Should they stay in the church?

Answer: Heavens Yes! They are all your spiritual children, even though they were exposed to the (familiar spirits). But whenever you are preaching and teaching, especially around them, remember that you also have special ones inside your congregation that were, (spiritually tampered with) and if you do not use the name of (Jesus Christ of Nazareth) you and these children are always going to be in a "spiritual warfare", which can be avoided if you only use the name of Jesus Christ of Nazareth!

Should Women Be Allowed to Preach and Teach the Gospel?

Caution: Bishops and Pastors "Must" always remember, these are God's children not yours or mine. We will have to give an account to God for whatsoever we do or did unto them, be warned!

1Samuel 15:22 And Samuel said hath the Lord as great delight in burnt offering and sacrifices, as in obeying the voice of the Lord? Behold, to obey is better than sacrifice, and to hearken than the the fat of rams.

Many Christians over the years are seeking to become highly spiritual, to become an intercessor. While this is great news that you are desiring to become a member of the prayer warriors team. We "Must" be ordained by God Himself first, God is the only one who can authorize you and I to become His spiritual lawyers Representing the Kingdom of Heaven government (God's word). You and I "Must" first study God's word to gain knowledge about His kingdom and how to operate inside of the spirit realm, in order for us to be effective against the kingdom of darkness. Whenever you and I are praying on the behalf of someone else, we will have to be extremely careful, or we will end up getting spiritual hurt, or loosing the soul of another to the kingdom of darkness.

Warriors "Must" know and understand that the only weapon we were given is the name of JESUS CHRIST OF NAZARETH. Yes! The mighty name of Jesus Christ of Nazareth, using anything other than the name of Jesus Christ of Nazareth is witchcraft and sorcery! How do I know this you maybe asking? Well as a former sorcerer, the main ingredients used in warfare was water, olive oil, and Florida water.

We have underestimate Satan's power to imitate or duplicate. Christian's are also ignorant of their own "Rights of the Spiritual realm" One of the common mistakes made by churches today is, Satan I rebuke you with the Blood of Jesus Christ, this is totally madness, while it may sound powerful, it is not. Those of you that desire to pray for someone, *start by practicing on yourselves and your family members first*. It is highly hypocritical to claim that you are *freeing someone else, when you too are spiritually bound, and need to be delivered yourself, how can prisoners free prisoners?*

Wait on God to purify and set you free first. So many of the people today who claim that they are spiritual discerners are only using wisdom and not The Spirit of Truth, Jesus Christ of Nazareth. *If you are claiming to be a spiritual discerner and you must look into the eyes of individuals to determine if they are possessed with demons, then you are nothing but a trickster working with the spirits of witchcraft!* I have seen this type of behavior before, even Bishops and Pastors I have seen using wisdom, while (practicing) witchcraft, "Obeah" as we Jamaicans would say. Those persons who are rebuking demons using the "Fire of God", those demons are only playing around with you. What do I mean? Demons can sacrifice themselves of their power, just to keep you and I in spiritual bondage! God only ordained the mighty name of Jesus

Should Women Be Allowed to Preach and Teach the Gospel? Christ of Nazareth, for you and me to use, nothing else can rebuke demons, only the name of Jesus Christ of Nazareth. Lucifer is not afraid of these names and titles!

- The Blood of Jesus Christ.
- The Fire of God.
- The Name of big brother Jesus, did you know that this is one of Lucifer's titles, "Big brother Jesus."

How stupid can we become, Jesus Christ of Nazareth is not our brother, even though He was in the flesh, Jesus Christ of Nazareth was indeed God inside the flesh, our God! Lucifer and all his demons, are afraid of the name of Jesus Christ of Nazareth, take it from a "former employee of Hell, until God save me by the name of Jesus Christ of Nazareth." A TRUE TESTIMONY.

Chapter Five

Should Women Be Allowed to Preach and Teach the Gospel?

This chapter is personally dedicated to Prophetess Shonyah Hawkins-Cottman, My Editor and Friend, who helped to make this book possible: aka "Shining-jah" light in Darkness!

To God Be The Glory, In the Name of Jesus Christ of Nazareth: Now Unto the Women Arise!

For centuries this question has been the focus inside our churches. Why? Why would Paul teach that women should keep silent in the churches, does this apply to us today? Should women really keep silent in our churches?   The first thing we should understand is that there were personal problems that were taking place in Corinth.   Bishop Paul from headquarters had to write a personal letter, address to the Corinthians and not the whole body of Jesus Christ of Nazareth! When I consider all the women throughout the scriptures and those we encounter today that God has filled with his Holy Spirit and anointed to preach and teach his word. Are they to truly remain silent?   Family of God, we are here to learn together, no motives, or hidden agendas even if they want to keep silent, The Holy Spirit inside wouldn't allow them to, believe me.

> "For God is not the author of confusion, but of peace, as in all churches of the saints. 34 Let your women keep silence in the churches: for it is not permitted unto them to speak; but they are

Should Women Be Allowed to Preach and Teach the Gospel?
commanded to under obedience also saith the law
(1Corinthians 14:33-34)."

The true meaning of these two verses. *God who rules and governs heaven alone, sent His Only Begotten Son, Jesus Christ of Nazareth, to save the church. God didn't save His church to have undisciplined Corinthian women causing wars and behave like it is a "fish market" inside the church. Therefore, I Bishop Paul commanded that all the women of the church of Corinthians, be kept in silence because they were hardheaded, and rude. I know that I am not wrong either for saying this, because even our laws that were given by our Prophet Moses support me. From now on let every Bishop and Pastor of all the churches of Corinth, keep your unruly women silent in the church. Other churches do not behave and operate like you! Do not consider for a moment that God is a part of your folly or even supports it, because God is not the author of confusion!* 1 Corinthians 14:12 tells us, "Even so you since you are zealous for spiritual gifts, let it be for the edification of the church that you seek to excel." After all, only what we do for Christ will last! Let the women teach, preach, evangelize, give prophecy or whatever spiritual gifts they have if that is what God has commissioned and assigned them to do. But, I must hastily say this is not an attack on Paul! I do not know all the circumstances surrounding why he would write that women should be kept silent in these churches of Corinth. But I strongly disagree with these types of behavior inside our church today, even though

63

there is enough evidence to support that we are the ones who misunderstood Bishop Paul! I am not religious, neither am I self-governed, I am only a "Representative of the government of Heaven"! I am only a son of God who questions this type of religious belief and practice within the body of Jesus Christ of Nazareth. To all you bigots inside the body of Jesus Christ of Nazareth: I can understand when the "world disrespect or even disregard our foundation of the family" (women). But when this is done within the body of Jesus Christ of Nazareth, I, Spair Lee, stand against this and any other imprudent thinking or behavior toward our women in the church or at home. Treating these women with little or no respect at all is against the very heart of God. God hold you accountable for this. To some of you women, who accept this garbage from us men, **STOP IT!** Do not sleep with the enemy for you are royalty! My sisters, it is time you learned and understand who you are in Christ! Yes, God made men first, and?? Did you know that even though Men are considered the head, it is the women who are considered as the brain, have you ever seen a head without a brain, or a brain without a head?

Why are we so eager to belittle each other, male or female, aren't we all sinners at the foot of the cross, we are all save by the mighty name of Jesus Christ of Nazareth, "classified as children of God and not agendas of God!" Stop allowing the enemy to make us feel, accept, or behave less than what we are and should as a woman of God; a Daughter of the King! Yes, God made man first.

Should Women Be Allowed to Preach and Teach the Gospel? Did God tell Adam to let the women be silent? 1Peter 3:7, "Likewise you husbands, dwell with them according to knowledge, giving honor unto the wife, as unto the weaker vessel, and as being heirs together of the grace of life; that your prayers be not hindered." You see, it did not say anything about women keeping silent in God's sight. We are all equal. Likewise, the bible states in 1Peter 2:9, "But ye are a chosen generation, a royal priesthood a holy nation, a peculiar people: that ye should shew forth the praises of him who hath called you out of darkness into his marvelous light." The record shows us that Paul boasted on himself at times and we believed that he was single. I will not take advice from any unmarried man who has not either experienced what it is like to be in a committed relationship or who does not respect God commission given to men concerning women! This is just my own opinion!

Genesis 1:27 So God created man in His own image, in the image of God created He him; male and female created He them.

Today, we are living in a civilized world, and ministering to the lost souls are far more important than fighting over agenda. Yet! there are still some men with living among us with cave-man mind set. To all those fools, who think that women are less, or lease important to our state, or even worse inside our churches today. The other day, I read one of the most ignorant posts; I believe I have ever read published on face-book. Such madness! Mike

65

wrote a post, calling women dead, and describing them as blasphemers, all because he believed that God does not recognized women prayers: this is not only disrespectful; but degrading. It is total garbage.

1 Peter 2:9 reads, "But we are a chosen generation, a royal priesthood, a holy nation, a peculiar people, that we should shew forth the praises, of him who hath called you out of darkness into his marvelous light." The true meaning of this verse?

I am God; I am the only one who runs things in Heaven and in earth all by myself! When you all sinned against me, I could have just kill off everyone, but because of my promise to Abraham, I send my only begotten son Jesus Christ of Nazareth and save you! Whenever you accept Jesus Christ of Nazareth, you automatically become a priest unto me! And because Jesus Christ of Nazareth is Holy, you become holy, because Jesus Christ of Nazareth is a king, you are automatically Royalty, you are now representing Myself and my son in this dark world that you are living in walk in my words and my marvelous light will guide and protect you. Where in the bible, did it mention that God react to a gender of male or female? We are all children in the sight of God, and God only responds to faith: Hebrew 11:1 reads, "Now faith is the substance of thing's hope for, the evidence of thing's not seen." Women are our equals in the sight of God! To all you cave-men, get this through your thick skulls; we don't need your stupid ways inside the body of Jesus Christ of Nazareth. Women are not our

Should Women Be Allowed to Preach and Teach the Gospel? possessions, our sex toys, our slaves, or ours to control. If anyone of you bigots have a problem with this, then you should consult or take it up with God! All you bigots, didn't you have a mother? Why then are you so disrespectful to women? Today, some of these jack-asses have brought the same attitude into our churches, showing little or no respect to our women.

John 3:16 reads, "For God so loved the world that he gave his only begotten son, that whosoever believeth in him should not perish, but have everlasting life." What are you trying to teach to our females, that they are followers, and not leaders? Are you trying to show them that their place is inside the kitchen, and making babies' or doing dirty laundry? To all those men who have a personal issue with woman being Teachers, Pastors or even Apostles of the Gospel of Jesus Christ of Nazareth, your issue is not with these sisters; but with God! What!? God is the one who has filled them with the Holy Spirit. Joel 2:28 tells us, "and it shall come to pass afterwards, that I will pour out my spirit upon all flesh and your sons and your daughters shall prophesy. Your old men shall dream dreams and your young men shall see visions. The true meaning of this verse.

When Jesus Christ of Nazareth came and died on the cross, this will quench my anger! So after Jesus Christ of Nazareth spend three days and three nights inside hell, I God: will raise him up, and take him back besides me in Heaven, and anyone who accept Jesus Christ of Nazareth, will be able to see in the spirit realm,

67

and speak of everything that they see while in the spirit realm: everything that I chose to show them in vision and dreams. I God have spoken it. I told you, your issue is with God! Now if I know anything about God, one thing is certain no flesh can dictate to Him. I don't care who you are, what position or title you may have, you cannot tell God what to do!

To all the Sisters of the household of Jesus Christ of Nazareth, You couldn't keep quiet if you wanted to anyway. How do I know this? Jeremiah tried it and even he could not hold it, you see, he was angry with God at one point in his life. But no man or woman can hold fire in their bosom without being burned. Jeremiah 20:9 tells us, "then I said, I will not make mention of him, nor speak anymore in His name. But, his word was in my heart as a burning fire, shut up in my bones and I was weary with fore bearing and I could not stay." Ladies! Because you were made equal in the sight of God, through the blood of Jesus Christ of Nazareth, God now responds to your faith and not to your gender. Now faith is the substance of things hoped for and the evidence of things not seen (Hebrews 11:1). Men are busy killing off each other and wasting themselves in clubs and mischief that God has responded to the cry of the weeping Mary and poured out his Holy Spirit upon them and sent them into the vineyard; truly the harvest is ripe, but the labors are few. God had to fill the Sisters with His Holy Spirit to feed His spiritually starving children. Jeremiah 20:10, tells us, "For I heard the defaming of many, fear

Should Women Be Allowed to Preach and Teach the Gospel?
on every side. Report, say they, and we will report it. All my familiars watched for my halting saying, peradventure he will be enticed, and we shall prevail against him, and we shall take our revenge on him." God's people are spiritually malnourished, while mankind is busy defaming our Sisters' Characters! God had to keep all those weeping Rachels whose crying and mourning for the children of this dark world and equip them with the Holy Spirit of Heaven through His Only Begotten son Jesus Christ of Nazareth. But Why? Mothers are natural care-givers, they know exactly how to feed and nurture for their young. It is in their nature, both physically and spiritually. Prophetess Shining-Jah light in Darkness, continue to do the work of our Father in Heaven, in the Name of Jesus Christ of Nazareth!

Chapter Six

Spiritually Gifted

To God Be The Glory, In the Name of Jesus Christ of
Nazareth: Now Unto the Proud of Heart
Message: Who or What Is Our Greatest Enemy?

For years, I was of the belief that Satan and his entire hosts were my greatest enemies; but I was so dead wrong. Even though Satan and is host are one of my enemies, they are not my greatest enemy! Then who are our greatest enemies SpairLee? Our **own self pride**! Yes! We are our own greatest enemies and the deadliest weapons against our own souls! Did you know that the strongest and worse demon to battle against is called self-righteousness? Believed me whenever these spirits come upon you: not even God can help you! Until the individual see that he is wrong and choose to repent, God have to reject him but why? Simply: He is the one who first rejected God!

1Samuel 15:26 And Samuel said unto Saul, I will not return with thee: for thou hast rejected the word of the Lord, and the Lord hath rejected thee from being king over Israel. The true meaning of this verse? *Well Saul, how can you be so stupid to try and fight against the one who have your life in His hand, how dump can you be? But worse, he is the one who owns the people of Israel, because they are stiff-necked and force God hand, that is the only*

70

reason why you were selected king over His People Israel in the first place. And now you have caused His People to sin against Him, by walking in the spirit of witchcrafts, Saul only He alone can help you now, but you are so stupid, before you run back to Him for forgiveness, you come to me! What can I do?

If you rejected God, and He in return rewarded you back with your rejection, please don't get me involved. What is it that you are thinking inside, that I have powers of my own to dictate to God? God is the one who ordained me a Prophet, so I answer to Him, I cannot help you in this matter, you are on your own!

After accepting Jesus Christ of Nazareth, as my personal Lord and savior, I realize that whatsoever power Satan once had over me was now broken! Satan is very intelligent and deceptive, but he has no power over the body of Jesus Christ of Nazareth: After the birth, death and resurrection of Jesus Christ of Nazareth, Satan was strip of his powers! If we say that Satan is the one who owns evil, then we are also implying that he is the god of evil; if he then be the god of evil, this would mean that God would be a liar, as there would be two Gods! A God for Good! And a God of Evil! But we know by nature, and with every fiber of our beings, that this is not possible, even before we receive The Spirit of Truth, we come to know and understand that it is not inside God's nature to lie. Then who used these powers against us? The truth is, we are the ones who have been using these powers against ourselves, by choosing to walk in the spirit of disobedience. Did you know that

71

the spirit of disobedience brings a curse? This is why, it may appear that God is responsible for it, when the truth is, it is our poor choices! God gave Mankind power over His creations, and over their own Spiritual and physical destiny! But we choose to walk in curses instead! Rather than accepting the blessings that God had intended for us! Genesis 3:1, "now the serpent was more subtle than any beast of the field which the LORD God had made. And he said unto the woman, yea, hath God said, ye shall not eat of every tree of the garden?" The true meaning of this verse; Now Lucifer at that time was God smartest creation, he was so intelligent but deceptive, because of his deceptive nature, God had to describe him as a snake, but why? Well a snake is the only creation of God that have one head and one tongue that split at the ending, which means that Lucifer can take the Truth and twist it into a lie! The splitting at the end of his tongue, representing double standard, incapable of telling the truth and confusions!

My brothers and Sisters, Jesus Christ of Nazareth is now The Tree of life standing in the midst of this world, eat of him, (accept Him) we shall not die Spiritually again but live forever. Credit these Revelations to The Holy Ghost, they are just popping up inside while I am writing. God is the one with both Good and evil in his hand, it is very important, that when we his children come into His presence, we must be clean on the inside. Why? God can best be described as a mirror, SpairLee what are you saying? A mirror only reflects what is place before it, this mean if we are

72

Good, God reflect "Righteousness upon us"! But if we are Evil, then God reflect "Unrighteousness upon us"! This means that we are our own judge; God is only a reflection (rewarder) of what He sees inside our souls!

God cannot choose for us, neither can He rewarded us Good or Evil! God can only reflect what He sees inside us, Good or Evil! Galatians 6:7 tells us, "Be not deceived; God is not mocked: for whatsoever a man soweth, that shall he also reap. We were created free moral agents with the ability to choose our own destiny. God cannot force us inside Heaven or Hell. We are the ones who make that choice! Therefore, we are our own greatest enemy, not God or Satan but Mankind!

Galatians 6:7 Be not deceived, God is not mocked: for what-so-ever a man something, that shall he also reap.

This paragraph is not for everyone, in fact, this is only for those of you who know deep down inside of you, that you are spiritually gifted, ordained by God Himself. Yes, it is for those of you who have been getting some visions and do not quite understand them. Yes, it is also for those of you who were spiritually alive and doing well after you accept Jesus Christ of Nazareth as your personal savior! But now you are finding it hard to even worship the same way you did when you first started out. Now it seems as if you are spiritually dead, or worse, spiritually bound or stagnant. *God had blessed me with the spiritual gift of discernment and authorized me to identify all His Fallen Prophet's and Prophetesses and restore them back to their former glory, in the name of Jesus Christ of Nazareth. God wants you to know and understand that He is still in charge, be encouraged and know that our Father is still in control, in the name of Jesus Christ of Nazareth!*

Are you under spiritual attacks? Are you perplexed and pressed down on every side? Continue to read the pages of this book, these words that are written within are for God's glory through Jesus Christ of Nazareth, and to uplift while encouraging you His people! On May 10, 2015, I was invited to a church in Clarendon by one of my sisters of the household of faith! The Pastor was overseas, and he had received message that God's word was not going forth from the pulpit. He wanted to get someone else's opinion about what he was told about his church! When we arrived at the church, I was greeted by the prince of the atmosphere, yes; the spirits of darkness were waiting for our arrival. Being a former wizard, I had expected this! Satan has his stronghold in every major Town Parish and major Communities where people are residing! But what had me perplexed was why the devil would use a Pastor's church to setup his stronghold? Spiritually this was taboo! Unless this church didn't belong to God in the first place! When I was introduced to the woman who was believed to be the person in charge, immediately, The Holy Spirit revealed her as the witch of the church and community! This witch was now the one left in charge to offers up spiritual sacrifices unto God! How can you give a witch or wizard the responsibilities of

God church? Did you know that our temple represents God's plate, and our prayers and Praises represent His Spiritual food?! Now how can someone leave a sorcerer with such sensitive responsibility, unless this Pastor was one of the following:

One, spiritually bound or Spiritually Dead!

Two, the church belongs to Lucifer, or Lucifer and this church are friends; either way, God was not in total control! Sister D, my prayer partner at the time and I had to spent hours praying, and rebuking demons out of their church before we could get some sleep. That Sunday morning, during worship service, God showed up and the Holy Spirit lifted a standard, it was then, that we could all see those that needed spiritual Deliverance! All the leaders were at the top of the list, their leaders were all demonized. The Evangelists and Missionaries were all demonized! I thought at first the Pastor too "Must" be demonized! If the body is spiritually sick, then it is an indication that it is coming down from the Spiritual head! I asked Sister D to make an appointment for me with the Pastor, who happened to be her biological cousin. To God be all the glory in the name of Jesus Christ of Nazareth.

May 24, 2015 while I was worshipping with the Pastor, I realized that this man was a bowl of hot air! Yes, he was very eloquent but lacked the presence of The Holy Spirit, it was evidently clear that this man wasn't even ordained by God! *He was not anointed, not appointed, and not sent by God*! Yes, he was displaying a spirit, but it wasn't The Holy Spirit! There was nothing holy about it either, the spirit that this Pastor was now manifesting can be found in 2 Corinthians 11:4 "For if he that cometh preacheth another Jesus, whom we have not preached, or if you receive another spirit, which you have not received, or another gospel, which you have not accepted, you might well bear with him." The true meaning of this verse. Listen to me now clearly, if anyone else comes up to you and starts telling you about another Jesus Christ, don't believe him, because I, Bishop Paul, have come to the knowledge and understanding that there are some people who started to worship, "Lucifer Jesus Christ," and trying to mixed him up with "Jesus Christ of Nazareth," so be careful. Even though this spirit is "almost identical like Jesus Christ of Nazareth," you will know the "Difference" between both, by the new messages that they will be preaching. Lately it is called "prosperity messages." That gospel only speaks about earthly riches and refuses to speak about suffering and hell today, but I, Bishop Paul tell you that this new gospel is going nowhere, so it is better if they choose to suffer with us now, for at least we know that our suffering soon ends, but their own will just start! That Pastor may be the one in charge of that church physically, but it was evidently clear that sister J was the one offering up Spiritual sacrifices unto God! Which he spewed out of His mouth!

Revelation 3:15-16 tells us, "I know that works, that thou art neither cold nor hot: I would thou wert cold or hot. 16 So then because thou art lukewarm, and neither cold nor hot, I will spue thee out of my mouth." The true meaning of this verse. *I, God, personally know of you. I accepted your invitation after you invited my presence, but when I tasted your food (Praises,) I realized that it was neither cold (you don't know me personally) nor hot (you don't want a relationship with me). When I accepted your invitation you didn't even take the time to really learn me, instead you were caught up with chasing Spiritual signs and wonders. Now I will spue you out of my mouth. Why? Because if I continue to eat your praises, it will cause me to vomit up my stomach "wrath" upon you and all your generation. It will become a generational curse, just get out of my presence until you are ready to repent!*

It was only a matter of time before she and those demonic spirits of witchcraft would over throw him and take away all his earthly possessions by spiritual force! This is now one of Lucifer training center, recruiting the souls of mankind to the pit of "Hell"!

Few year's later, I was contacted by Sister D his cousin who told me that the Pastor was now confine to a wheelchair and Sister J had now moved in with the Pastor in his marital home. Now this was sin at its finest peak, as Sister J had now left her own husband! Can you believe that "allegations" had surface that the Pastor was now sharing his matrimonial home, with sister J living in a section of the house, while his wife is in another section of the same house! Listen very carefully, this is what these spirits of witchcraft does, it wrecks and messes up every perfect thing that God had intended for His human family. Yes, there were multiple marriages mentioned in the Bible of olden days, however; everything was done according to the will of God and in order. How do we know this? God is a God of order. To God be all the glory in the mighty name of Jesus Christ of Nazareth!

Chapter Seven

Marriage God's Way

To God Be The Glory, in the Name of Jesus Christ of Nazareth: Now Unto the Husbands and Wives Inside The Church! Message: God Hates Divorce!

I became sexually involved with my wife long before we decided to get married in October 2010. We were both backsliders at the time but, I was now attending church very regularly, so we thought that it was now appropriate for us to get married. I told my bishop at the time about our relationship, I explained to him that we were sexually active, and I had no intention of leaving her. I wanted him to understand that I would continue attending church but, I would not take part in any activities until we are both officially married. This was the topic of the bishop's sermon the following Saturday. This man had spoken over the microphone everything that we had spoken about during the week. Well, pride got the best of me and to be honest, I was very upset with him at the time for his poor choices. Spiritually, I was now dying again! To God Be All the Glory, In The Mighty Name of Jesus Christ of Nazareth! Saturday October 30, 2010, my girlfriend and I got married; we were in love with each other and we both wanted to make a fresh start with God: After deciding that we both needed a place of worship, we made the decision together to return to the bishop's church. Our

Pastor at the time hosted our wedding ceremony at his home; his wife was one of our marriage witnesses. Immediately, after our marriage ceremony, the Pastor's wife was the first to place curses over our marriage. Can you believe that this woman told my wife she could file for a divorce within two years and remarry if she wanted to. The worse part of this was the fact that I was still standing there before her as she spoke these words.

After the ceremony, we went to the church that I had backslide from, as this was a part of our marriage agreement! The bishop was the next person to curse our marriage, "Ahab just married Jezebel today and now they are both here to take over my garden," referring to his church as his garden. When the bishop's wife heard that I was now married, she was not pleased at all. Why you ask? When I was sixteen years old, her sister was my childhood love, so when I joined their church everyone thought that I was going to marry her, only then would I be accepted as a member. My wife was washing her hands at the pipe side, when the bishop's wife approached her, "Are you mad?" she asked my wife.

It all started out innocently enough, for years whenever people would see us together for the first time and ask who was the good one. I would tell them that my wife was my better half. Nothing was wrong with a statement like that, but when I started to label her as my earthly god, that is where I went wrong. Wow, believe me, my wife started to display authority over me in our marriage, she was now behaving like the man, but it didn't stop there. I was now being disrespected at home and now even while we are out in the public at church. The words that I had spoken into the atmosphere were now manifesting itself in our marriage.

One day I cried out to God, God's simple reply, "You are the one who said that she was your earthly god, you are the one who gave her the dominion over you!" Immediately, I prayed about this situation, but the damage was already done. Things began to change for the better after I prayed, but looking back now on those days, I should have spent more time in prayer and fasting! Why? Years later, God reveal that my wife was now my idol or god and I was the one who placed her so. I learned from God that he was the only one who could remove my idol. My God, I had to beg God night and day to remove her: I had placed my wife where God was supposed to be in my life! My God, I even got mentally ill over her at one point. You see, June 2015, I found out that my wife was seeing someone. She would tell me that she was going to stay at her parent's house, this was her meeting point, and I felt like I was going to die. My God, believe me there were times when I felt like my heart was going to stop beating.

What I was feeling for this woman, I had never felt it before, not even for God. Can you imagine, God was the one who gave me life and here I was being ungrateful unto Him? My God, I was now displaying more love for my wife than for God, let me explain? I would go days without even praying but, I would see my wife every single day. There were days when I had to walk miles, because I didn't have any bus fare just to see my wife, I felt helpless or compelled to see her. I knew something was wrong but, I just couldn't seem to stop myself from seeing her. It was only when I beseech God in prayer and fasting, this spell was broken. My God, I was the one who had set up this idol but, God was the one who removed it!

Exodus 20:3-4 Tells us, "Thou shalt have no other gods before me. Thou shalt not make unto thee any graven image or any likeness of anything that is in heaven above, or that is in the earth beneath or that is in the water under the earth." My God, I am the one that is responsible for killing our marriage. It was my stupidity, God could have killed us both or each of us one after the other, at any time. It would have been justified too! When we met six years earlier, everyone who knew we were together said that she was going to leave me in the future; to be honest, I was wondering the same thing too but, when I got the vision to marry her, I did. My wife's relatives hated the thought that we were married. They believed that I wasn't good enough for her, and this wasn't any secret, when she became confused, she wanted us to visit a marriage counselor! "Honey, please, we need to see a marriage counselor." My reply to her was always, "Baby we are ok." "Honey, I do not know my responsibilities as your wife, Glen please." This was her desperate cry for help. We were both living together when we got married. Our Pastor at the time told us that marriage is like living in a common law relationship, so he didn't see any reason for us to be seeking marriage counseling. My second mistake! I listened to this nonsense.

My wife started to work in the downtown area; there she became sexually involved with one of her co-workers. She was now using her parent's house as a meeting point, every weekend she was now visiting her parents. When God reveal this to me, in a vision, what was going on, I confronted her about it. We had a heated argument, I was the one who told her to go, I was hurting deep inside and I didn't want to let jealousy get the best of me, she moved out of our marital home! My wife called me about 2:00am on a Wednesday morning few hours before daybreak, my God: I was so excited, "Glen meet me downtown Kingston." She was in tears over the phone begging my forgiveness. My mother and sister were the ones who got the call and handed me the phone, wow, when I heard her voice immediately my world was alive again:

Wife: "Glen!"

Glen: "Yes baby"

Wife: "Glen I am sorry for all the pain and disrespect that I caused and put you through."

Glen: "Baby it is ok. We all make mistakes."

Wife: "Yes Glen, but how could I be so stupid to fall for that lie?"

Glen: "Baby we all make poor choices sometimes, you are here now."

That morning I was up very early, my God, I was so excited and happy; I was like a child who had not seen their parents for a long time. When she arrived I hugged her, then we boarded a bus heading to Montego Bay. For most of the journey we were both in silence, we were just holding each other's hand. When we arrived in Montego Bay, I called my cousin and he told us which taxi to take to his home. See, when my wife called that morning, I immediately ask my cousin if we could spend some time at his home, away from everyone and everything. I explained to him that we needed to be alone to work on our marriage.

Now Satan wasn't going to give up without a fight, one night we were about to go to bed, it was late, and my wife was still on her phone. "Baby, please put your phone away and spend some time with me, please." I reached over and took the phone from her hands, my God; my wife was now transformed into a different person. I saw my wife appearance and behavior change immediately. Wow, she was now breathing heavy but short, she began to act wildly. The crazy part, was watching her trying to climb the wall back ward. This wasn't strange to me as a former sorcerer, I had seen it before on many occasions, but it was affecting me more watching my own wife act and behaving this way. I immediately started to cry while praying, "Father, God in the name of Jesus Christ of Nazareth, Father I beg you, this is my wife, in the name of Jesus Christ of Nazareth, save her please God." A few minutes later my wife was asking, "Glen, what just happened?" She explained that she couldn't seem to remember anything; I told her what happened but reassure her that we are going to be ok. After our two weeks had ended, my wife got a vision one morning and told me that God said it was time now to go back home to our matrimonial home. Amazingly, she was the one refusing to return home in the first place! When we came back home, my wife didn't want to leave the house. She said that she wasn't ready to face our neighbors. "Glen I am not going to suffer with you any longer, I did enough already." "Baby, remember that God said we should hold on just a while longer." "Yes Glen, but I am not going back through that again."

One morning while we were still in Montego Bay, my wife got up and told me that God said, "Everything is going to be ok." She was the same one who told me that God said our breakthrough was very, very, near: I believe God was the one speaking to her at the time. Why? I got a similar vision also confirmed what; she was now telling me! Then my wife got a song in her vision, as if God had given her a written covenant. *The words of the song:*

Thou the battle maybe hot and the conflicts though rocky the road as we travel along hold on a little longer, hold Jesus Christ of Nazareth at His word and he will carry you through to the promise Land.

When I realized that my wife was determined to leave me again, I started to bury myself in work. A few months earlier, I went mentally ill over her and now that I let her back in, history was about to repeat itself. At this point I didn't know what to feel, deep inside I wanted to hate her, confusion and anger were my closet friends.

One Thursday morning, my wife and her friend decided to take a trip to St Thomas. Honestly, I didn't want her to go, but if I had tried to stop her, maybe it would have caused world war three, worse, it would have proven to her that her relatives were right. They told her that I was monitoring her and that she needed to make her own mistake. I was working on the roof of our church when both came in, my wife called to get my attention; if I remember correctly, they were both smiling:

Wife: "Glen, later"

Glen: "Ok," I replied. Then they went through the church doors. Can you imagine, of all the places on earth, these two decide to deceive me in the place where we all worship the previous Sunday! When my wife didn't call or came back home that night, I went to the church yard where my wife friend and family were staying. I asked the friend's husband if she was home, it was then that I learned everyone inside the church was aware that my wife was leaving me. My God, to be honest I was so deeply hurt inside, and I was so ashamed. Wow, why is it always the hurting person who is the last to find out what is going on?

One day while I was praying in tears, Father, I cannot handle this situation any more, my heart, wow, my heart felt like I was about to die. I honestly didn't think that I was going to make it, I couldn't breathe. The very air that I breathed with her was now leaving me. Father in the name of Jesus Christ of Nazareth, God, are you going to let this killed me? I felt the very hand of God hugging me. I had felt this touch before when I first got saved. I could hear God speaking to my spirit, "let her go," this was truly between her and God. Few weeks later, my wife called me beseeching me to let her go. "Glen let me go, please, let me go!" She said, "Glen your innocent wife is dead, she is not coming back home, let go." I began to plead with her, "baby, remember you are the one who called me, I don't even know where you are." With a chilly voice she said, "Glen, God is telling me that I should come back home, so this means that you are praying for our marriage, Stop! Just let me go and move on with your life." The only reason I offer you the reader this testimony is to encourage anyone else going through or facing a divorce. I want you to know that you can make it. I SpairLee went through it already and Yes, I made it, so can you!

"Father in the name of Jesus Christ of Nazareth, as we your people come back to you in repentance, in the name of Jesus Christ of Nazareth. Father we pray that you will wash us in the blood of Jesus Christ of Nazareth, cleanse us and use us for your own glory in the name of Jesus Christ of Nazareth, Amen."

Romans 7:2 For the woman which hath an husband is bound by the law to her husband so long as he liveth; but if the husband be dead, she is loose from the law of her husband.

Question: Is it ok for someone to remarried after a divorce? This is a very serious matter and should not be taken lightly. Yes, it is ok if you are having marital problems and choose to separate or even divorce! But be it known, God will hold you accountable for this or any other choices that you and I have made! God hates divorce! But, He will not and cannot force two people to live together. Even though it was God who blessed my marriage and confirmed it, He couldn't force my wife to stay with me when she had chosen to leave! When my wife and I were going through our separation, I seek the intervention of a well-known Pentecostal Church here in Jamaica. My God! When they learned about my background of being a former "sorcerer," they taught my wife that it was ok for her to withhold sex from me, and this is expected to force me to go "Sex Hunt" then she would be free to divorce me on the account of "adultery", and then she would be "Free" to marry again! But wasn't this teaching and beliefs morally wrong and "Devilish?" Well this was the teaching and counseling session my "then wife" received, no wonder my marriage didn't have a chance, "Satan" use his (this Pentecostal) church to end it! According to the Pentecostal church doctrine, the person that cheated first is bounded by the law, while the next is free to marry again. No wonder the divorce rates are so high among "church goers", note that I said church goers, and not God's people! If you are separated from your matrimonial home, for God sake, try and work on your marriage. "Dating other people at this time is morally wrong!" Divorce must be your last option, but if the person chooses to leave, open the door yourself and let them go! Never try to force someone in staying with you, "Never", even if they stayed with you, your life is going to be a living hell. Why? They are going to disadvantage you, and they have every right to, because you are the one who force them to be there in the first place! When my wife left, I was "Instantly famous." Everyone seems to be talking about me, passing all sorts of "negative remarks" about me! My God! But just look at me now, I am glowing in God's presence and His glory. Since, I have chosen to walk in Obedience unto God, through His Only Begotten Son Jesus Christ of Nazareth: These blessings have nothing to do with me; God is the one who is responsible for all these blessings and my sanity today!

To God be all the glory in the mighty name of Jesus Christ of Nazareth!

Chapter Eight

Spiritual Warfare: Rules and Regulations

To God Be The Glory,

In the Name of Jesus Christ of Nazareth:

Now Unto the Prayer Warriors!

Message: How to Pray and Get Results.

I have been teaching in steps intentionally, emphasizing on the importance of the name of Jesus Christ of Nazareth. The reason for this is to prepare all those Christians who are seriously living for God and brave enough to stand upon the behalf of their fallen brothers and sisters as prayer warriors! *Rules and Regulations were made to govern, and they are expected to be kept! The same way we keep and follow laws governing the natural realm, we must also do it in the Spirit realms.* If these laws and rules are not observed and kept, then the prayer warriors can find themselves in contempt of court: And find themselves in serious trouble with the presiding judge who happened to be "God Himself"! Yes, God is the judge that presides over this Spiritual Court! But why? God is the only one faithful and just enough to give a fair judgment: God is the one who makes these rules and regulations in the first place! We all know that God is all powerful and almighty, well this is true: but we should also know that God is a God of order. *It was God who made these laws and rules to the spiritual realms in the*

90

first place, and not even God Himself can break one of them! We are not greater than our master, if he can observe them and keep them, then we are expected to also observe them. Satan knows these laws and rules, therefore he can beat the unsuspecting Children of God, because they do not know their rights and are ignorant about it too. Mark 1:23-24 tells us that Satan was inside the church raising "havoc." In fact, he was now a resident inside the church! "And there was in their synagogue a man with an unclean spirit: and he cried out. Let us alone; what have we to do with thee thou Jesus Christ of Nazareth? art thou come to destroy us? I know thee who thou art, the Holy One of God." Verse twenty-four depicts another side of Satan, here Satan is revealing unto us who and what he is afraid of. Yes, you got it right! It is the name of Jesus Christ but look at the sequence in which Satan used the name. He did not just say Jesus or Jesus Christ but, **Jesus Christ of Nazareth**.

Many prayer warriors fail to observe this, resulting in a spiritual warfare and even worst yet, not having their prayers answered! When you are praying on the behalf of someone, Satan will be coming straight at you the prayer warrior! Why? Satan already has the fallen individual and you are now getting involved, you are now his next target! All of us have our own beliefs of who we think Jesus is or a version of who we think God is. Prayer warriors, I beseech you, whenever you are praying on the behalf of someone! First, begin by introducing them to the Jesus Christ that you are talking about! Some demons are dumb, deaf and blind, this means that you will have to pray aloud: for example: Father, in the name of **Jesus Christ of Nazareth as I come to you in prayer on the** behalf of "call the person name that you are praying for" in the name of Jesus Christ of Nazareth! That was a short Example of how your prayers should always be addressed, anything else will "linger in the atmosphere." Why? Simply: You didn't "stamp it with the only approved stamp of Heaven." What? Not what but who? Yes, the name of "Jesus Christ of Nazareth: is not only a saving name. It is also a spiritual stamp" that governs the three "Spiritual Kingdoms' and all these "kingdoms' governments" knows and accepted this stamp! What "kingdoms' government" are you talking about Spair Lee? One (1) *Heaven's Kingdom Government*: Isaiah 9:6 For unto us a child is born, unto us a son is given: and the government shall be upon his shoulder: and his name shall be called Wonderful, Counselor, The mighty God, The everlasting Father, The Prince of Peace. This is "Heaven's Government" system being introduced unto us by God Himself! Two (2) the government of earth! Genesis 1:28 And God blessed them, and God said unto them, be fruitful, and multiply, and replenish the earth, and subdue it: and have dominion over the fish of the sea, and over the fowl of the air, and over every living thing that moveth upon the earth. This is "Earth government" being introduced to us by God Himself! Three (3) The government of Hell: Matthew 25:41 Then shall he say also unto them on the left hand, depart from me, you cursed, into everlasting fire, prepared for the devil and his angels. This is "Hell's government" being introduced to us by God Himself! Jesus Christ of Nazareth his now "The Head of the Government" of all these "kingdom's governments"! How did Jesus Christ of Nazareth become "The Leader" over these kingdoms government? There was a World summate and all those other "kingdoms' government" chose Jesus Christ of Nazareth as their world supremacy? Where did this World Summate Delegation took place that decided which Kingdom government would govern the "Third and Forth Dimensions of the Spiritual Realms"! Where was it held? Way back in "Heaven," but finalize in Pilate Hall and their weapons and powers was displayed and established on Calvary cross! Revelation 5:1, 7 And I saw in the right hand of him that sat on the throne a book written within and on the backside, sealed with seven seals. 7 And he came and took the book out of the right hand of him that sat upon the throne. That day on Calvary's cross when all the three "Crucified Jesuses were representing and defending their own "kingdom government"! Spair Lee you are mad, what are you talking about? Well, that day on Calvary's cross they were hanging three Jesuses, each one representing the different "kingdom governments" that was now being represented! Prayer warriors, never assume that the person who you are praying for knows God personally, even if they are of the faith. *Prayer warriors never allow the individual that you are praying for to open the spiritual realms upon you*! What do you mean? Always be the one first to pray around the individual you are praying for and if they are praying: then emphasize that they use the name of Jesus Christ of Nazareth as often as possible inside their prayers! Why? To avoid any unnecessary spiritual warfare between you the prayer warriors and the individual that you are praying for! Remember that you are there to help these fallen brothers and sisters in the first place and not to fight with them spiritually causing more damage! Prayer warriors, I beseech you, do not become high minded: God is the one "Delivering the individual not you"! *Prayer warriors remember that some demons are called Jesus and Jesus Christ*; this means that you "Must always use the name of Jesus Christ of Nazareth! And that they are praying in the name of Jesus Christ of Nazareth as well! Warriors, never be in much hast to lay your hands on the individual, before you know and understand what you are dealing with first. Why not? All spirits are transferable, Good or Evil!!!!!

1 Corinthians 11:13-15 For such are false apostles, deceitful workers, transforming themselves into the apostles of Christ. 14 And no marvel; for Satan himself is transformed into a angel of light. 15 Therefore it is no great thing if his ministers also be transformed as ministers of righteousness; whose end shall be according to their works.

I have been teaching you about the name of Jesus Christ of Nazareth.

Spiritual Warfare: Rules and Regulations

Question: What new doctrine is this?

Answer: This is not a new doctrine, in fact even the elders in Jesus Christ of Nazareth time ask this same question! Certainly, there is nothing new about this, you are just using the correct name! Yes! The mighty name of Jesus Christ of Nazareth! Mark 1:27 And they were all amazed, in so much that they question among themselves, Saying, What thing is this? What new doctrine is this? for with authority commandeth he even the unclean spirits, and they obey him. The title of our Lord and Savior Jesus Christ of Nazareth was intentionally place upon his cross! Have you ever wonder why? God knew that Lucifer was a "copycat," he can only fabricated things. He is not able to create anything! He is only capable of "Inventing things" God created church family! "Lucifer Invent Religion"! God designated Jesus Christ of Nazareth as our personal "Spiritual Robe," Lucifer copied this also. Therefore, our church today is being "Invaded by men wearing dresses" calling them preaching robes! This is a lie from the pit of Hell, those materialistic robe are worn by "Satanic high priests they are a copy version" of the "Original Robe" who is Jesus Christ of Nazareth! God is now separating His Church out of these churches! God is now gathering His chosen "Soldiers": God's army is now recruiting loyal soldiers for the final battle; Yes! This battle ground will determine who will be saved! My brothers and sisters are you a member of God's army? God has been gathering His People

95

from all over the world. This process will continue until all God's Chosen people are on board!

Revelation 3:9 Behold, I will make them of the synagogue of Satan, which say they are Jew's, and are not, but do lie; behold, I will make them to come and worship before thy feet, and to know that I have loved thee. To God All The Glory, In the Mighty Name of Jesus Christ of Nazareth!

Question: With so many churches in the world today: How can we identify The True Church?

Answer: The True Church will be using the name of Jesus Christ of Nazareth regularly: Every Kingdom and Nation have their own flags or symbols: "The Heavenly Kingdom Flag is the name of Jesus Christ of Nazareth! God's True Church as already put on their "Spiritual Robe"! Yes, the name of Jesus Christ of Nazareth: this is the only Robe that God Himself had design and issue to His Holy Church for our "Spiritual Robe" Yes! the name of Jesus Christ of Nazareth!

Matthew 24:5 For many shall come in my name, saying, I am Christ; and shall deceived many.

Children of God: The Antichrist spirits are already here upon us, and they have invaded our churches. These are people who have signed a legion's unto Lucifer, and today they are known as Satanic worshippers: These people are now calling demons Jesus or Jesus Christ: God is not the author of confusion! This is why God has saved me, a former sorcerer, and sent me back to declare His name among the His own people who have become a stranger unto God! God is forced to defend Himself and His Church!

> 2 Corinthians 11:13-15 states, "For such are false apostles, deceitful workers, transforming themselves into the apostles of Christ. 14 And no marvel; for Satan himself is transformed into an angel of light. 15 Therefore it is no great thing if his ministers also be transformed as ministers of righteousness; whose end shall be according to their works."

The simplest translation of this verse. The Antichrist spirits have recruited their own workers of darkness and placed them inside our Churches today. These Satanic worshippers are now operating from our Churches' pulpits: As Bishops and Pastors polluting and perverting our gospel with fabricated lies! But this action doesn't surprise me because their father Satan also change himself to copy our Lord and savior Jesus Christ of Nazareth! Who is "The True Light of this dark world": To God be all the glory in the mighty name of Jesus Christ of Nazareth!

Question: Why his God doing this?

Answer: God had no choice, He was forced to protect His Holy name! God have to remain faithful and blameless! If he fails to defend His church, then we will have all right and reasons to blame him for not identifying Himself unto us properly: for us to be able to identify Him personally, different from the Antichrist spirits which also is identical in appearance; but not in substance!

Question: When should we start wearing this Robe? Immediately after we received Jesus Christ of Nazareth as our personal Savior!

Revelation 3:9 tells us, "Behold, I will make them of the synagogue (church) of Satan, which say they are Jews, and are not, but do lie; behold, I will make them to come and worship before thy feet, and to know that I have loved thee." The simplest translation of this verse. Listen unto me carefully, *I am a God of Holiness, you are claiming to be a representative of me with your stupidness! You cannot please me with your sorcery spirit, yet you refuse to repent and change your evil ways! Listen unto me clearly a day is coming, when you are going to bow down upon your knees before me, by will of choice or forcefully! And when you learn of me and realize that I am a loving Father, then you will fully understand my true love for you!* Philippians 2:10 states: That at the name of Jesus every knee should do, of things in heaven, and things in earth, and things under the earth. The Antichrist spirit is here, and it has invaded our church: God words are being fulfilled right in front of us each day. We cannot push this aside any longer, it is here and our only protection against this is the name **Jesus Christ of Nazareth!**

Question: Why are we in this mess?

Answer: To fulfill prophecies, it is a "Must that God words have to be fulfilled": And The Church of God failed to follow God's instructions and choose to walk in disobedience!

Question: What instructions?

Answer: Even in the human family we have learned how to honor our parents. We dare not call our parents by their first name, yet we do this with God! God calls us as children not adults, therefore we "Must" respect and honor Him. Malachi 1:6 tells us, "A son honoureth his father and a servant his master; if then I be a Father, where is mine honor? And if I be a master, where is my fear? Saith the Lord of Hosts unto you, O priests that despise my name. And ye say, wherein have we despised thy name?"

Ephesians 6:2 tells us," Honour thy father and mother; which is the first commandment with promise; That it may be well with thee, and thou mayest live long on the earth." In this way we also must honor God! After all, He is the giver of life! He sustains us all and His grace is ever sufficient! Then why is our churches today seem so powerless against Satan's kingdom of darkness, as many Christians are living a defeated Christian lifestyle simply because they are ignorant of their personal Rights in the spirit realms! God is not dead, neither has He lost His powers, why is it then that God Church appear spiritually weak today? Doesn't God love His People anymore, has God changed? No! Hosea 4:6 tells us, "My people are destroyed for lack of knowledge: because thou hast rejected knowledge I will also reject thee, that thou shalt be no priest to me: seeing thou hast forgotten God, I will also forget thy children. The simplest translation of this verse. *My people love darkness and their own evil Ways more than my light, and righteousness! Therefore, they have refused to seek after my counsel and commandments: Because they have rejected my knowledge, I will also reject their self-righteousness! I will not allow them to be my priest, nor will I allowed them to offer up sacrifices unto me, now or in the future! Since they have no respect and regards for me, neither will I regard anything they tried to offer me! Neither from this generation nor their off spring to come!* Whenever we choose to walk in our own Counsel, immediately we breach our own Spiritual protection! Only God alone can offer us Spiritual protection, take it from me a former sorcerer! Numbers 22:12 And God said unto Balaam, Thou shalt not go with them: thou shalt not curse the people: for they are blessed. The simplest translation of this verse. *Listen unto me Balaam, I am tired of your greedy attitude, anyone I bless now or in the future, you or anyone else cannot curse them! Whenever I blessed anyone they are well bless and no flesh can stop it*!

A sorcerer or a fortune teller cannot give blessings or curses; this can only be done by God Himself alone. Why? *God alone governs the Spiritual realms, blessings and curses comes from God alone not Lucifer*! When I was working for Lucifer as a sorcerer, I was always of the beliefs that I was able to have offered blessings and Spiritual protections! During my practices as a sorcerer, many people would come seeking this Spiritual protection believed to being offered! Now that I have been fully delivered from the spirits of witchcraft: 1 now realized that this is only a myth! Then who is the one responsible for our blessings or cursing upon our lives? It is neither God nor Lucifer, but us! What? We are the ones who choose Spiritual blessings or Spiritual cursing?

Spiritual Warfare: Rules and Regulations

Whenever we disobey God: immediately we opened the spiritual realms negatively over our lives: Whenever this is done then the spirits of witchcraft are activated inside our lives!

Today many Christians are praying, and their prayers seems as if they are not being answered! But why? Many Christians today are unaware that they are an "ambassador" of Jesus Christ of Nazareth: Which mean that they are now a representative of the Heavenly kingdom Government: they need to know and understand that in order to carry out any "Official business" praying to God they will have to use the "Official Heavenly Kingdom stamp" the name of Jesus Christ of Nazareth! Why? Because this is an "Official matter on the kingdom behalf" they will have to use the "kingdom stamp" that they were given when they were selected for the position of an "ambassador." What do you mean SpairLee? As soon as we accept Jesus Christ of Nazareth as our personal savior, immediately we are given an "authorizing code" and an "Official stamp" for the kingdom of Heaven! What is this code? "Faith"! "What is this stamp"? "Not what, but who"? "The name of Jesus Christ of Nazareth"! When we use the name of Jesus Christ of Nazareth the Heavenly Government cannot refused "You and I Entrances" unto The Throne of mercies!

"With this Stamp, the name of Jesus Christ of Nazareth," we cannot be turned down or denied Entrances into the Kingdom of Heaven! Whenever the name of Jesus Christ of Nazareth: Is being called over our lives then we are sealed. Because we used the name of Jesus Christ of Nazareth our prayer requests are approved, and God is forced to answer our "applications forms"! The beauty about this "spiritual stamp" is, it is known throughout all the three spiritual realms and accepted by all the three kingdom's governments systems! "Heaven's Government knows and accepted its approval"! "Earth's government knows and accepted its approval"! "Hell's government knows and accepted its approval"! Romans 13:1 Let Every soul be subject unto the higher powers, for there is no power but of God: the powers that be are ordained of God. The simplest translation of this verse. Every human being that is upon this Earth is governed from the Heavenly Government kingdom throughout all the three spiritual realms! Both humans and angelical spirits: Good and Evil must live in subjection with the final decisions made by the Heavenly Government in the Spiritual realms! Only the Heavenly Government can override any decision or cancel any decision that was made in the spiritual realms! Once God pass down judgement inside the spirit realms, eartly government, or Hell's government cannot appeal the case! Furthermore, whenever we resist and rebel against God final decision, inside the spiritual realms! We will only set up ourselves to eternal condemnation and Death!

Any Christian praying and fasting is now on an "Official matter" concerning The Heavenly Kingdom, and the name of Jesus Christ of Nazareth "The stamp Must" be used at all times! On this or any "others matter" if you are praying on the behalf of someone else concerning the "Heavenly kingdom: You are expected to use "The Stamp" the name of Jesus Christ of Nazareth! Any "ambassador" Christian refuses to use "The Stamp" the name of Jesus Christ of Nazareth on matters concerning The Heavenly Government, Knowingly or unknowingly "Refusing to" call upon the name of Jesus Christ of Nazareth! Even if it is out of ignorance of not knowing their personal Rights in the Spiritual realms, then those prayers requests will not be answered! Why not? Jesus Christ of Nazareth said anything that we need from the Father, must be done in his name, Yes, the name of Jesus Christ of Nazareth. Once God hears the name of Jesus Christ of Nazareth! Yes! The name of His only Begotten Son Jesus Christ of Nazareth: Then He is going to responded back to you and me, because we've have followed the instructions of Jesus Christ of Nazareth.

John 14:13-14 And what-so-ever you shall ask in my name, that will I do, that the Father maybe glorified in the Soon. 14 If you shall ask any thing in my name, I will do it.

Many are called but few are chosen, only those that are spiritually gifted are able to pray on the behalf of someone who is believed to be possessed with a demonic spirit or a spirit of depression and release them from their spiritual prison. For each Christian's to be totally effective inside the spiritual realm, they must first Learn **about the rules** and regulations that were placed there inside the Spiritual by God Himself! They are there to govern the three spiritual Kingdom's and for our own personal protection inside the Spiritual realms! These rules and regulations "Must" be observed and kept at all times, not even God Himself can break one of these rules or change them! Let me explain: Jesus Christ of Nazareth said, "anything you ask of the Father in my, will be given unto you." That is the law and it cannot be changed. What are these rules and regulations? The words of God they are the rules and regulations of the three Spiritual realms! Matthew 24:35 Heaven and earth shall pass away, but my words shall not pass away. The simplest translation of this verse. I am a God of Holiness and integrity: I take pride in my words, they are my final decisions whenever I speak: I myself will uphold them, they are my Truth and Righteousness: keep them and you will live forever, disobey them and you will be lost forever! For us to have our prayers answered: Every Christian "Must" follow these rules and regulations. How? By following the instructions given inside our Bible carefully! Heaven is a place of order; therefore, we must ensure that we follow each instruction given! Heaven is a place that is governed only by the name of Jesus Christ of Nazareth! Every Christian praying for himself or on the behalf of someone "Must use" the name of Jesus Christ of Nazareth to get result from Heaven! And this rule and regulation was given only unto The True Church of Jesus Christ of Nazareth! "Once we use the name of Jesus Christ of Nazareth, in this same sequence: All the Spiritual realms "Must" obey the command that follow": And this is the law of the Spirit realms. John 14:13 And whatsoever you shall ask in my name, that will I do, that the Father may be glorified in the Son. The simplest translation of this verse? *Children of God: I am now back in Heaven with our Father: And I am the key to the store room: which is full of everything that concerns you while on Earth! Please my friends I beseech you: Ask whatsoever you need in my name: Yes! The name that is above all names: The name of Jesus Christ of Nazareth: And the Father "Must" response to you*! This is an example of how your prayers should be addressed unto God: Once it is addressed in this same sequence, God the Father "Must" reply unto you! Father, in the name of Jesus Christ of Nazareth: God as I come in the authority of the name of Jesus Christ of Nazareth: I need a job: "then you stamp it" in the name of Jesus Christ of Nazareth. God I need you to help me grow up spiritually: "then stamp" in the name of Jesus Christ of Nazareth: Amen. Whenever we know and understand these rules and regulations that govern the spiritual realms, then we will become more powerful, why? Knowledge is powerful! Whatsoever we ask God for in the name of Jesus Christ of Nazareth: God will grant it unto us if it is in line with His perfect will for our lives! Matthew 16:19 And I will give unto thee the Keys of the kingdom of heaven: and whatsoever thou shalt bind on earth shall be bound in heaven; and whatsoever thou shalt loose on earth shall be loosed in heaven. The simplest translation of this verse. My Father made all these things for my glory, all three kingdoms is mine! The kingdom of

Heaven is mine! The kingdom of Earth is mine! The kingdom of Hell is mine! I Am the Alpha and The Omega: I Am the First and The Last! I called them my Kingdom's because I AM the One who made them! Now I choose to share my authority and powers with you my Children: My name is the "Only Key" into these three Spiritual kingdoms: the name of Jesus Christ of Nazareth! And whatsoever that you requested in my name by faith, Shall be done unto you now, And shalt in the future: And whatsoever you decide to be free upon the earth now and in the future, as long as it is in line with my "Words" and perfect will it shall be done as you command it: And then you will have "Heaven" approval: Because you use the name of Jesus Christ of Nazareth! To God Be The Glory, In the Name of Jesus Christ of Nazareth: **What Power Does A Sorcerer Have Over Others Or The Church?** This is a very great question, but to answer this question we will have to find out what is "Sorcery"!

Sorcery is the manipulation of one's mind: "A Sorcerer and magicians are able to influence and control someone mind through the power of illusions and Witchcraft"! Anyone who can control our minds is working with the spirits of "Witchcraft"! "This is why God gave you and I the knowledge to govern and choose our own destiny He didn't want to control us"! Now let us see what the words of God said about this! Galatians 3:1 O Foolish Galatians, who hath bewitched you, that you should not obey the truth, before whose eyes Jesus Christ hath been evidently set forth, crucified

106

among you? The simplest translation of this verse. *Stupid People living in Galatians, how can you be so Foolish to allowed wizards and witches to put a spell upon you.* Imagine this nation should be one of the first to live in "Repentance." This nation gets a "first eye views of the healing powers and miracles of Jesus Christ of Nazareth": And how he was falsely accused and condemn to death by way of Crucifixion right here before your eyes: And yet you allowed these wizards and witches working in the "spirit of disobedience and illusions to capture your mind and spirit while leading you astray"! But all hope is not lost. If this nation will repent and return to their former state: When they first saw those miracles and healing done by Jesus Christ of Nazareth, based upon 2 Corinthians 10:1-5 All Spiritual strongholds and spell can be broken and pulled down in the name of Jesus Christ of Nazareth!

> 2 Corinthians 10:4 -5 For the weapons of our warfare are not carnal, but mighty through God to the pulling down of strong holds: 5 Casting down imagination's, and every high thing that exalteth itself against the knowledge of God, and bringing into captivity every thought to the Obedience of Christ;

The simplest translation of this verse. God is a Spiritual being who control and rules the universe from Heaven: He is the only sources that can fight against any Spiritual strongholds over our fleshy desire: Therefore let us put God in control over our lustful and deceptive minds: If this is not done, then you and I will become high minded: boastful because this is just the nature of our flesh:

God hates competition and whenever flesh act in rebellion against God and refused to retain God in their knowledge, He withdraw Himself and allow you and I to have our way which leads to Hell: Let us behaved ourselves wisely then and walk in the spirit of Obedience unto God, in the name of Jesus Christ of Nazareth!

I have been fully delivered and walking in total obedience unto God through His Only Begotten Son Jesus Christ of Nazareth! "The three Spiritual realms are now fully open up unto me: The Heavenly realm! The Earthly realm! And The Hell realm! They are all now at my command, through the name of Jesus Christ of Nazareth"! "With all this knowledge and understanding of the spiritual realms": I am still able to do "witchcraft and black magic": And I am dead serious, so I will explain! Many people are of the beliefs that whenever you are saved, and delivered that God clears your mind of all your past activities. Well, that did not happen to me! God save and fully cleansed me, but he did not take my memories away from me: No! Instead God taught me how to operate more matured inside the spiritual realms! But I am the one who choose not to return to the "realms of witchcraft"! Why not? While I was working as a sorcerer: I was spiritually blind unto the things of God! Why not?

Psalms 25:14 The secret of the Lord is with them that fear Him; and he will show them his covenant. The simplest translation of this verse. God is a Counselor all by Himself. He does not take advices from Wizards and Witches: Even though they self-claimed that they are able to foretell the future there are no guarantees: Worse! God hate opposition and He do not share His glory! Only when we become humble and dependable upon God: Only then will God show us all the goodies that He has to share with us, whenever we choose to walk in His perfect will, in the name of Jesus Christ of Nazareth!

This is also confirmed by King David in the first chapter of Psalms one! Psalms 1:1 blessed is the man that walketh not in the counsel of the ungodly, nor standeth in the way of sinners, nor siteth in the seat of the scornful. The simplest translation of this verse. God can only bless us whenever we choose not to seek advice from Satanic worshippers: Wizards and witches cannot sit at God counseling session: Neither are they God's friends: They are like vomit before His presence! God only share is knowledge and intentions with His friends: While you and I choose to walk in rebellion against God: We automatically become God enemies: My brothers and Sisters would you tell your enemies your secret? This is the same way with God: He hates sins; but "Love sinners" Romans 1:22 tells us, "Professing themselves to be wise, they became fools." The simplest translation of this verse? *Wizards and witches are representing the kingdom of darkness and working with the spirits of lies and deceptions: Even though they are hearing from the spiritual realms: They are fools because only God alone can foretell our future. Why? God alone governs and controls the spiritual realms, not Lucifer or mankind!* Now that

God save and cleansed me: I am now able to sit at God Counseling session with Him: Now I can see on both sides of the three spiritual realms: Good and Evil are open unto me! The main reasons why I Spair Lee choose to remain faithful and loyal unto God!

(1) I am now a friend of God through Jesus Christ of Nazareth!

(2) I am now able to fulfill my true purposes upon this Earth: in the name of Jesus Christ of Nazareth!

(3) Whenever my time here on earth is expired and I am laid to rest: God will reward me for all the works that I had done while here on earth, in the name of Jesus Christ of Nazareth!

Today, I am best described by Genesis 3:22 "And the Lord God said, behold, the man is become as one of us, to know good and evil: and now, lest he put forth his hand, and take also of the tree of life, and eat, and live forever." The simplest translation of this verse? God said Behold SpairLee has become as one of us, he now knows and understand the three spiritual realms: I will now place my only Begotten Son Jesus Christ of Nazareth: In the center of his life that he will now be a representative of "The Heavenly Government" while on Earth, and I God will reward him with everlasting life! Did you know that whenever someone got saved and delivered that those demons still visit them every now and again! Why? When I said those spirits still visit them, notice, I did not say that they are in charge of them: they only visit, to see if they are still walking with God. Now if I should ever one day

110

backslide, then all those spirits would take over again, and worst, they would go and get seven stronger demons, to ensure that they do not loose me again. Why? They need back their old master and finding a clean vessel to live, they wouldn't want to give it back. I must rebuke demons, daily just to remain spiritually clean each day! In April 2011 when I was going through my season of trials, there were times when we couldn't even find work. Ask God how he did it because if you ask me, I will end up lying to you. But we never went to bed without food and our bills were paid. All through this Satan was telling me you can come back and work for me; I will take care of you. You see, I was approached by a well-known Bishop who asked me to stay besides him and things would be ok. This Bishop is now one of Jamaica's largest Sorcerer and high priest. One day his wife told me, "With your Jesus Christ of Nazareth and with our "Jesus Christ" we can make a lot of money. Immediately! God separated me from him to save my soul and keep me spiritually clean! One night I got a vision about this Bishop, when I told him what was revealed unto me in the vision, "Tell God where I live," he said, "doesn't God knows my address. Tell God to bring me the message Himself," mockingly while refusing to repent.

One day when my wife and I were still living together: I choose to walk in disobedience against God's will. The Bishop wife was aware that my wife and I were hungry and struggling at the time. The Bishop's wife called and asked if we would like something to eat. Now one would think that this was a righteous gesture. But it wasn't! You see, the Bishop wife knew about the warning that I had gotten from God. She offered me and my wife five hundred dollars ($500) and something to eat! She deliberately tempted me with the food, and the money: I was dumb to have accepted it! Knowing that God had already part us from him! The Bishop's wife thought that she would have me under her control: As she is believed to be a known witch! As soon as I received that money I Immediately knew something was wrong spiritually! For several days demons filled our home: And the only reason we are alive today is the fact that I have a personal relationship with God! The last night before I received my break through; I had a vision seeing a witch trying to kill me spiritually. In the vision I was rebuking her in the name of Jesus Christ of Nazareth; repeatedly. The witch died spiritually that night; at this point I was spiritually free. From then my wife and I made God a promise, we'd rather die of hunger than to "SOLD" him out like that again! My question to you is; what or to whom; did you sold Jesus Christ of Nazareth? Judas did it for thirty (30) pieces of silver; I did it for a plate of food and five hundred dollars! To God be all the glory in the mighty name of Jesus Christ of Nazareth!

Chapter Nine

Revealing the Three Jesuses

To God Be the Glory, In the Name of Jesus Christ of Nazareth

Now Unto the Churches

Message: Revealing the Three Crucified Jesus

"Did you know that every Church has their own Jesuses"? Over the years, God has taught me that every church has their own version of "Jesus or Jesus Christ." These so-called churches call demons or evil spirits, "Jesus" and "Jesus Christ." To be honest, most of these people don't even know who or what they are worshipping. Many people today, both here in Jamaica and overseas are worshipping demonic spirits and calling these satanic spirits, "Jesus" or "Jesus Christ." Some do it and are very much aware that they are, while others have no clue.

> Jesus said unto her, woman believe me the hour cometh, when ye shall neither in this mountain, nor yet at Jerusalem, worship the father. 22 Ye worship, ye know not what: We know what we worship: for salvation is of the Jews. 23 But the hour cometh and now is, when the true worshipper shall worship the father in spirit and in truth: for the father seeketh such to worship Him. 24 God is a spirit: and they that worship Him must worship Him in spirit and in truth (John 4:21-24).

In most of my posts on Facebook and other social media forums, I have tried to reach few churches along with Bishops and

113

Pastors in a bid to share God's knowledge with them. These so-called churches may appeared to be normal on the surface, but do not be fooled by these so-called miracles and promises of Visa permits to the USA, these desires and empty promises opening the spiritual realm to Satan himself. How would I know this? This is a very good question; I was once a Satanic High Priest and very active one too, until God saved me in December 2004. I was on my way to prison by my former girlfriend when I met God. Today I am very grateful unto God for giving me another chance. Young men, God is real! Young ladies, God is real! He is a God who gives second chances. Today satanic worshippers in Jamaica have changed their appearances. Once we could have easily identified them when they were wearing their colorful uniforms. Today Satan has changed his appearance, but he is using the same evil spirits. Even though these so-called churches are harder to identify with the natural eye. If you have a personal relationship with God, then these satanic churches will not easily deceive you.

> "For such are false apostles, deceitful workers,
> transforming themselves into the apostles of Christ.
> 14 And no marvel; for Satan himself is transformed
> into an angel of light. 15 Therefore it is no great
> thing if his ministers also be transformed as the
> minister of righteousness. Who then shall be
> according to their works?" (2 Corinthians 11:13-15)

Now that I have pointed out the problem, here is the only way that we God chosen vessels can begin to fix it. "Satanic worshippers and demonic spirits are afraid of the name of Jesus Christ of

Nazareth. They cannot use the name of JESUS CHRIST OF NAZARETH in this same order or sequence". They will call our Messiah:

1. Lord Jesus
2. Jesus Christ
3. Jesus

"Did you know that there are three Jesuses represented inside our Bible?" They are as follows:

1. Jesus Christ of Nazareth represents the saving of Mankind. John 3:16 tells us, "For God so loved the world, that he gave us His Only Begotten Son, that whosoever believeth in him should not perish, but have everlasting life.

2. Barjesus, who is also called Elymas; represent the Devil, or destruction of the world. Acts 13:6, tells us "And when they had gone through the isle unto Pathos they found a certain sorcerer, a false prophet, a Jew whose name was Barjesus." The simplest translation of this verse? And when they come to a certain place: Barnabas and Paul see a spiritualist: working with the spirits of "Witchcraft": He is pretending to be a part of our Church: He is a member of a so-call church; Even though his name is called Jesus, he is not "God only begotten Son Jesus Christ of Nazareth!

3. Jesus of Justus represents Mankind and the "Pride fullness of this world that he struggles with daily". Colossians 4:11tells us, "And Jesus, which is called Justus, who are of

the circumcision, these only are my fellow workers unto the
kingdom of God which have been a comfort unto me."

The simplest translation of this verse?

Here is another Jesus, he is called Justus: All this Jesus is
concerned about is the things of the flesh. Now you and I know
that flesh cannot please Almighty God! This Jesus is only
concerned with the pride of Life! 1 John 2:15 tells us, "Love not
the world, neither the things of the world. If any man loves the
world, the love of Father is not in him." It is evidently clear then
that this Jesus represent Mankind! Gen 3:22 tells us, "And the
Lord God said, "The man has now become like one of us, knowing
good and evil; and now, lest he put forth his hand, and take also of
the tree of life, and eat and live forever." You see, the devil has
supernatural power, so does man and God. God, because of his
love for us, didn't want us to experience the demise of faith that
Lucifer experienced, in fact God wants us to worship like him to
ensure our fate with him.

When mankind chooses to accept Lucifer's lies as, the truth,
immediately, we became like the gods inside the Spiritual realms.
Gen 3:22, "Behold the man has become like one of us." This
means we became immortal in the spiritual realm. With this
knowledge a powerful man became like the gods. The phrase, "to
know good and evil, unless man puts forth his hand to take of the
tree of life, putting the flesh to death," meant that God, knowing
the plans He had for us, decided to put man out of the garden.

Why? Flesh had to die on the cross to settle the price of sin accumulated by Adam and Eve immediately after they had sinned against God.

Romans 3:23,"For the wage of sins is death: but the gift of God is eternal life through Jesus Christ our Lord." We see the plan of God begin to unfold when God sent Moses to Egypt. God knew that man had their own perversions of power called magic. Do you recall the story of Moses visiting Pharaoh on the behalf of children of Israel, petitioning Pharaoh at the request of God, to "Let my people go?" To make clear to Pharaoh that God was the one speaking, and that God was in fact "God," Moses was instructed by God, to throw down his Rod, which became a serpent. It was then that Pharaoh sent for his magicians and sorcerer. He wanted to exercise or display his own Powers. You see, mankinds power is known as magic and that is why they are called magicians. Why did the Rod of Moses transform into a serpent? This was on open show: God wanted mankind to understand that Jesus Christ of Nazareth, is far more powerful than "Lucifer the serpent" who caused Adam and Eve to sin against God.

> "For in Him dwelleth all the fullness of the Godhead bodily. 10 And ye are complete in him, which is the head of all principality and powers: 11 in whom also ye are circumcised with the circumcision made without hands, in putting off the body of sins of the flesh by the circumcision of Christ (Colossians 2:9-11).

To feel power is the pride of life. How do we know this? Because in the garden of Eden, when God called forth Adam after the fruit was eaten, Adam, realizing he was naked, feeling humiliated and prideful, sewed unto himself fig leaves and made themselves loin cloths. Immediately, after disobeying God's words, Adam and Eve knew that they had lost their spiritual coverage. They knew instantly that there was a breach or breaches in their relationship with God: So, Adam and Eve tried desperately to repair these breaches: How? By sewing fig leaves together trying to mend back or replace their Spiritual coverage, which can only be placed or repaired by God. Isn't it ironic that even though God has restored our relationship with Him through the "Birth, Death, and Resurrection" of His only begotten Son Jesus Christ of Nazareth. Even though Jesus Christ of Nazareth was "Resurrected from the Dead" and now sitting in Heaven on the right hand of God the Father, mankind is still trying desperately to repair these breaches. How, by sewing unto themselves material cloths calling them spiritual robes. Why? Simply because we refuse to accept the "True Spiritual Robe" that God created for us. What are you saying Spair Lee, many of our Bishops and Pastors today are still doing the very same thing that Adam and Eve did. What? These men have sewed unto themselves dresses, calling them preaching robes, why? Simply because they are stiff-necked and operating in the spirit of disobedience and witchcraft against God. They are refusing to wear the only "Spiritual Robe" that was "Created by

God Himself" out of a "Rock." Yes! Jesus Christ of Nazareth is now our "Spiritual Robe" and covering created by God Himself?

Yes, it is the name of Jesus Christ of Nazareth. He is now our new covenant and only spiritual covering that connects us back to God. It was God himself who had created this "Spiritual Robe" but how and when?

> "And he said, thou canst not see my face: for there shall no man see me, and live. 21 And the Lord said, Behold, there is a place by me, and thou shalt stand upon a rock: 22 And it shall come to pass, that I will put thee in a cleft of the rock, and will cover thee with my hand while I pass by (Exodus 33:20-23)."

Throughout Biblical history, we were taught that Jesus Christ of Nazareth was the only one that was called the "Rock." This Spiritual covering is even better than the first one, How so? We are not only able to communicate with God, but we are now able to "touch God" through Jesus Christ of Nazareth. Hebrews 4:15 For we have not an high priest which cannot be touched with the feeling of our infirmities: but was in all points tempted like as we are, yet without sin. Genesis 3:11, " And he said, who told thee that thou wast naked? Hast thou eaten of the tree, where of I commanded thee that thou shouldest not eat?" Please note that:

1. The Power of God is called Holiness.
2. The power of the Devil is called sorcery.
3. While the power of man is called magic or magician.

119

Now based on Isaiah 42: 8, "I am the Lord; that is my name: and my glory will I not give to another, neither my praise to graven images." God does not share His powers, or His glory. God had to dethrone the devil and Mankind. That is why they were put to open shame on Calvary's cross, which was the final battle. **The first battle took place in Pharaoh's hall**.

> "When Pharaoh shall speak unto you, saying Shew a miracle for you; then though shalt say unto Aaron, take they rod, and cast it before Pharaoh, and it shall become a serpent.10 And Moses and Aaron went in unto Pharaoh, and they did so as the Lord had commanded: and Aaron cast down his rod before Pharaoh, and before his servants, and it became a serpent. 11 Then Pharaoh also called the wise men and the sorcerers; now the magicians of Egypt, they also did in like manner with their enchantments.12 For they cast down every man his rod, and they became serpents; but Aaron's rod swallowed up their rods (Exodus 7:9-12)."

The final battle took place in Pilot's Hall, but the battle ground was Calvary, the final games played on the hills of Golgotha, the hill of skulls. What is so significant about this battle? This battle, this game on the hill of Golgotha, was ordained. The Bible says in Romans 6:23, "For the wages of sin is death; but the gift of God is eternal life through Jesus Christ (of Nazareth) our Lord." The death of our savior had to take place in such a terrible place. Mark 15:22 tells us, "and they bring him unto the place Golgotha, which is being interpreted, the place of a skull. And they gave him to drink wine mingled with myrrh: but he received it not." This

120

was the final show down!   Based on this information, the hill of Golgotha, was now representing God's Holy Hill. Lucifer thought that he had won the battle, the kingdom of men was now under his control, and he thought that he had put Almighty God to an open shame.

All hope seems lost, Lucifer intentions were simple, he wanted to turn God's Holy Hill into a dry spiritual desert, spiritual deadness. How do I know this? Psalm 121:1 I will lift up my eyes unto the hills, from whence cometh my help. But wait a minute, Jesus Christ of Nazareth is not dead yet. Jesus Christ of Nazareth is saying something. John 19:30 When Jesus therefore had received the vinegar, he said, It is finished: and he bow his head, and gave up the ghost. Our debt of sin was now settled. Jesus Christ of Nazareth paid far more than enough, but why? If we stumble and fall into temptation and sin against God, grace and mercies are still in the account of Life to pay for our pardon and restore us back to him, in the name of Jesus Christ of Nazareth.

After they brought our Savior to Golgotha, they tried to force him to drink wine mixture with myrrh, the same scent, which was offered and received at his birth. What is the significance or meaning of this, mankind was now trying to make an open mockery of Jesus Christ of Nazareth. My God, we were the ones who presented him with these gifts at his birth, now we are using them against him. After Lucifer was forcefully evicted out of heaven into the earth, he realized that his angelic spirit powers

121

were no match for God. Lucifer decided to deceive Adam and Eve and then team up with them. They were both innocent at the time, Why? Lucifer thought that with his angelic powers and the breath of God, identified in Adam and Eve, he was now sufficient enough to overthrow God. Mark 15:23-24 And they gave him to drink wine mingled with myrrh: but he received it not. 24 And when they had crucified him, they parted his garments, casting lots upon them, what every man should take. Based upon these scriptures and verses, they brought our savior to Golgotha and try to force him to drink wine mixture with myrrh but why?

1. The wine was now representing the beginning of miracles and ministry of Jesus Christ of Nazareth.

2. The myrrh was now representing the ending of his time and ministry upon earth, in the flesh; which includes his death and burial.

Lucifer and mankind really thought that Jesus Christ of Nazareth was now out of the picture, they were now mocking him hanging there from the tree that was once representing light and life; but was now the tree of death and accursed. Jesus Christ of Nazareth, our Lord and Savior, was still alive. They were now trying to embalm him while he was yet still alive and travelling through hell in the Spiritual realm. Jesus Christ of Nazareth is saying something else, in John 19:30 When Jesus therefore had received the vinegar, he said, it is finished: and he bowed his head, and gave up the ghost. My God, Jesus Christ of Nazareth was the one who choose to give up his "Spirit." My God, Lucifer nor mankind couldn't kill him. It wasn't the pain and agony that he went through but, he chose to die to settle the payment of our sinful fleshy desire. Why didn't God leave us to die or receive the same punishment as Lucifer? Even though Adam and Eve had disobeyed God, they didn't know Evil at that time. God, being the just and loving God that he is, chose to give us another chance. Now that we have learned about good and evil, God will now judge us equally as Satan.

Mark 15:24 "And when they had crucified him, they parted his garments, casting lots upon them, what every man should take." When they crucified Jesus Christ of Nazareth, they took his garments, ripped them apart, sharing the glory; Mankind in choosing to rebel against God and His righteousness decided to work and live for the devil. Lucifer was now in total control; mankind becomes a servant of the devil. "Which of us will run the earth right now? You helped me to kill him." The devil claimed the souls of men and mankind that day, the possessions of life, the pride of life, all within a few seconds! Gone! The third hour they crucified him, three days and three nights shall Jesus Christ of Nazareth, stayed in the "belly or pit of hell" (earth). Three days and three nights Jonah was in the belly of the fish, third hour, because I am the Alpha, Omega, the beginning and the end. Jonah 1:17 Now the Lord had prepared a great fish to swallow up Jonah, And Jonah was in the belly of the fish three days and three nights.

And the subscription of the accusers was written over his head, King of the Jews. And with him they crucified two thieves. The three Jesuses are on the cross. One thief on the left and another on the right? Why? So that Jesus Christ of Nazareth, the sovereign man, the man who bored the stripes, would be the man in the middle. You see, the devil represented on the left and mankind on the right. The scripture was now being fulfilled. Why? They were label as the two thieves, because when Lucifer had fallen from God's grace and was placed upon the earth, he teams up with mankind and tried desperately to steal the kingdom of heaven from God, yet another time while he was now on earth. Lucifer and his angels tried to rob Adam and Eve of their true inheritance, the Garden of Eden. Lucifer actions forced God to put an end to his lies and deceptions which now ended up on Calvary, on the hill called Golgotha or skull, "city of the dead," for the final battle!

The thieves were claiming that they had the right to steal their rightful positions in the kingdom, but both the Father and the Son were being glorified. Remember the disciples asked in

> Matthew 18:1-4, "At The same time came the disciples unto Jesus, saying, "Who is the greatest in the kingdom of heaven?" 2 And Jesus called a little child unto him, and set him in the midst of them, 3 And said," Verily I say unto you, except ye be converted, and become as little children, ye shall not enter into the kingdom of heaven. 4 Whosoever therefore shall humble himself as this little child, the same is greatest in the kingdom of f heaven."

These are the teachings of our Savior! Even with all that Jesus Christ of Nazareth showed, ministered, and taught, the people as that passed by as he hung on the stake, wailed upon him; they were in support of his death. Shaking their heads and saying that, "thou hast destroyed the temple." Even then, they were more in tune with what they wanted, than what God wanted. They wanted to preserve the physical temple instead of the spiritual temple that Jesus Christ of Nazareth represented. Thus, the prophecy was fulfilled. 2 Timothy 3:5 "Having a form of godliness but denying the power thereof; from such turn away.

All the first born of God the Father have the right to use the name of Jesus. What am I saying? Let me clarify, 1. Jesus **Christ of Nazareth** is the first born of righteousness unto God the Father. He is not only the begotten son of God the Father; but the true heir of the Father's inheritance. Colossians 2:9 tells us, "For in him dwelleth all the fullness of the Godhead body."

2. Lucifer or Satan is also the first born of God and is entitled to use the same title Jesus. Being once an angelical spirit representing light, he is also entitled to use the title of Christ. Lucifer's power is almost identical to Jesus Christ of Nazareth with one exception, Satan being an angelic spirit, used the name/title of Jesus and his heavenly power to transform into an angel of light, something Jesus Christ of Nazareth never had to do!

> 2 Corinthians 11: 4, 13-15, 4 tells us, "For if he that cometh preacheth another Jesus, whom we have not

preached, or if you receive another spirit, which you have not received or another gospel, which you have not accepted, you might well bear with him....13 For such are false apostles, deceitful workers, transforming themselves into the apostles of Christ. 14 And no marvel; for Satan himself is transformed into an angel of light. 15 Therefore it is no great thing if his Ministers also be transformed as the Ministers of righteousness; whose end shall be according to their works."

3. **Mankind/human being**, we are also the first born of God the Father, this means that we are also entitled to use of the title/name Jesus. Being that we are earthly our powers are earthly and label by God as magical or walking in the spirits of sorcery's. Exodus 7:11-12, "Then Pharaoh also called the wise men and the sorcerer's: now the magician of Egypt they also did in like manner with their enchantments. 12 For they cast down every man his rod, and they became serpents: but Aaron's rod swallowed up their rods."

    Why a serpents? Serpents or snakes are the only living beasts or things created, by God the Father: with one head almost like unto the Father; but with one tongue spilt at the end, this is significant, why? The Devil is a liar and the truth is not in him!

    Genesis 3: 1-5 tells us, "Now the serpent was more subtle than any beast of the field which the Lord God made. And he said unto the woman, yes, hath

God said you shall not eat of every tree of the garden?
2 And the woman, we may eat of the fruit of the trees of the garden: 3 But of the fruit of the tree which is in the midst of the garden, God hath said, you shall not eat of it, neither shall you touch it, lest you die. 4 And the serpent said unto the woman, Ye shall not surely die: 5 For God doth know that in the day ye eat thereof, then your eyes shall be opened, and ye shall be as gods, knowing good and evil."

Satan was able to tell some of the truth; but notice, at the ending of his statement the spilt of his tongue activated; part of the statement true, part a lie." Physically they were still alive for a period: but immediately after learning about good and evil, they were both spiritually dead.

Revelations 12:7-9 tells us, "And there was a war in heaven: Michael and his angels fought against the dragon; and the dragon fought and his angels. 8 And prevailed not; neither was their place found any more in heaven. 9 And the great dragon was cast out, that old serpent, called the Devil, and Satan, which deceive the whole world: he was cast out into the earth, and his angels were cast out with him."

After Lucifer and one third of the angelic spirit powers failed to over throw God the Father in heaven, they were cast into the earth. Lucifer then sought out additional spirits and powers from the closest thing to God. Yes, a part of God's own self. When God created mankind, God entrusted man with a part of Himself. Genesis 2: 7, "And the Lord God formed man of the dust of the

127

ground and breathed into his nostrils the breath of life; and man became a living soul." My God! No wonder Lucifer is described as a serpent, did you know that a serpent will spend months or years starving itself, patiently lying in wait for its prey? Lucifer, was now trying to use God against Himself, What? Mankind was now deceived by Lucifer, getting ourselves involved in a war that didn't concern us. We now joined forces with Lucifer; fighting against God; using the gift God entrusted with, the breath of God. Why would we team up against God? Lucifer in return had given us a false promise to satisfy all our fleshy desire, for helping him to battle against God. Proverbs 27:20 "Hell and destruction are never full; so the eyes of man are never satisfied. After joining up forces with mankind, Lucifer withstood God for the second time, where? Right there in Pharaoh Hall: Satan thought that he was now more than ready again to challenge God. Lucifer loss the second battle against God again. "Then Pharaoh also called the wise men and the sorcerers: now the **magicians of Egypt**, they also did in like manner with their enchantments. 12 For they cast down every man his rod, and they became serpents: but Aaron's rod swallowed up their rods (Exodus 7:11-12)." God was now forced, to act against His two disobedient sons: Lucifer the angelic spirit being who called himself "Jesus Christ" and Adamic son called "Jesus". These two disobedient sons' in a bid, to over throw God their Father wasted their inheritances and almost ruining the perfect plan to God: their actions brought the kingdom a high death rate. God had to send His only begotten son, Jesus Christ of Nazareth; Son of righteousness to redeem honor back to Himself. Act 10: 38, "How God anointed Jesus Christ of Nazareth with the Holy Ghost and with power: who went about doing good and healing all that were oppressed of the devil; for God was with him."

God was deliberate in His actions. The first born of God, were all entitled to have their Father's possessions and the right to claim their fair share of inheritances. Lucifer, the first born angelic spirit being of God the Father, tried not only to claim all his inheritance, but decided to over throw God in the process. Understand this, God is a jealous God and will not be mocked or disobeyed! Isaiah 42:8, ''I am the Lord: that is my name: and my glory will I not give to another, neither my praise to graven images. 9 Behold, the former things are come to pass, and new things do I declare: before they spring forth I tell you of them. God was now force to settle the depths of sins: because of His two disobedient sons "Lucifer Jesus Christ" and "Jesus old Adamic nature" the debt price was so high that one was able to open the account book"!

> Revelation 5:1-10 tells us, "And I saw in the right hand of him that sat on the throne a book written within and on backside, sealed with seven seals. 2 And I saw a strong angel proclaiming with a loud voice, who is worthy to open the book, and to lose the seals thereof? 3 And no man in heaven, nor in earth, neither under the earth, was able to open the book, neither to look there on. 4 And I wept much,

129

because no man was found worthy to open and to
read the book, neither to look there on. 5 And one
of the elders said unto me, Weep not: Behold, the
Lion of the tribe of Juba, the Root of David, hath
prevailed to open the book, and to lose the seven
seals thereof.6 And I beheld, and, lo, in the midst of
the throne and of the four beast's, and in the midst
of the elders, stood a Lamb as it had been slain,
having seven horns and seven eyes, which are the
seven Spirit of God sent forth into all the earth. 7
And he came and took the book out of the right
hand of him that sat upon the throne.8 And when he
had taken the book, the four beast's and four and
twenty elders fell down before the Lamb, having
every one of them harps, and golden vials full of
odors, which are the prayers of saints.9 And they
sung a new song, saying, thou art worthy to take the
book, and to open the seals thereof: for thou wast
slain, and hast redeemed us to God by the blood out
of every kindred, and tongue, and People, and
nation.10 And hast made us unto our God king's
and priests: and we shall reign on the earth."

On crucifixion day, Jesus Christ of Nazareth was representing
God's Holiness, while defending God's government, honor and
Kingdom. Isaiah 9: 6 tell us, "For unto us a child is born, unto us a
son is given: and the government shall be upon his shoulder: and
his name shall be by called Wonderful, Counselor, The mighty
God, The everlasting Father, The Prince of Peace." Who were the
two accusers?

1. **"Jesus Christ, Lucifer"**, the angelic first-born spirit being
   of God the Father: Who was now representing his own
   selfishness and rebelliousness, his kingdom and the pit of

130

"Hell." He was on the left of Jesus of Nazareth. Proverbs 27:20 Hell and destruction are never full: so the eyes of man are never satisfied.

2. **"Jesus, old Adamic nature"**, the first born of God the Father. Who was now representing "Pride," his kingdom the world. He was on the right of Jesus of Nazareth.

1 John 2:15-16 tells us, "Love not the world, neither the things that are in the world. If any man loves the world, the love of the Father is not in him.16 For all that is in the world, the lust of the flesh, and the pride of life, is not of the Father, but is of the world."

Spair Lee, what you have described sounds theologically good, but is there Biblical evidence to support your claims? Yes! Here is the explanation of the three.

1) This is **Jesus Christ of Nazareth**, the only "Begotten Son of God" the Father: he represented God's Holiness.

Acts 4:10 Be it known unto you all, and to all the people of Israel, that by the name of Jesus Christ of Nazareth, whom ye crucified, whom God raised from the Dead, even by him doth this man stands here before you whole.

2) This is **Jesus Christ, Lucifer** he is also known as **"Elymas the sorcerer"** he is God first "Angelic Being" he represents "Destruction and Hell"

Acts 13:6-8 tells us, "And when they had gone through the isle unto Paphos, they found a certain sorcerer, a false prophet, a Jew, whose name was Barjesus: 7 Which was with the deputy of the

131

country, Sergius Paulus, a prudent man; who called
for Barnabas and Saul, and desired to hear the word
of God. 8 But Elymas the sorcerer (for so is his
name by interpretation) withstood them, seeking to
turn away the deputy from the faith."

3) This is **Jesus, also called Justus**, and he only cares for the
"Pride of Life" the things of this world that satisfied his fleshy
desire. Colossians 4:11 And Jesus, which is called Justus, who are
of the circumcision. These only are my fellow workers unto the
kingdom of God, which have been a comfort unto me. Now Jesus
Christ of Nazareth was given an unfair court trial. He was tried
without a lawyer or proper Representation on his behalf. He was
forced to defend Himself.

Mark 15:9-14 But Pilate answered them, saying, Will you that
I release unto you the King of the Jews? 10 For he knew that the
chief priest had delivered him for envy. 11 But the chief priest
moved the people, that he should rather release Barabbas unto
them. 12 And Pilate answered and said again unto them, what will
you then that I shall do unto him whom you call the King of the
Jews? 13 And they cried out again, Crucify him. 14 Then Pilate
said unto them, why, what evil had he done? And they cried out
the more exceedingly, crucify him. According to Pilate's
account, Jesus Christ of Nazareth was given an unfair court trial by
his two disobedient brothers': "Jesus Christ, Lucifer" and "Jesus,
old Adamic nature": according to the first born off spring titles.
Have you ever wonder why the focused, and emphasis was always

132

on the middle cross? Civilization as we know it starts in the midst or middle of the garden: the midst of the female body "garden" is called the womb; this is where fertilization take places thus start of civilization. "And out of ground made the Lord God to grow every tree that is pleasant to the sight, and good for food; the tree of life also in the "midst of the garden", and the tree of knowledge of good and evil (Genesis 2: 9)." "But of the fruit of the tree which is in the midst of the garden, God hath said, you shall not eat of it, neither shall you touch it, lest you die (Genesis 3:3). Therefore then, it is no mystery, Lucifer, having this knowledge, use his agent Achan back in Joshua's generation to plant an accursed seed in the midst or middle of the Israelite camp. "When I saw among the spoils a goodly Babylonian garment, and two hundred shekels of silver, and a wedge of gold of fifty shekels weight, then I coveted them, and took them; and, behold, they are hid in the earth in the midst of (Joshua 7:21)."

Today, Lucifer is using these same spirits/agents to mess up our church: the only difference between then and now, then they were called Achan: Today they are known as Bishops and Pastors: ministering unto us in the midst of the church from the pulpits or should I say, the "polluting-pit." God the Father had to place Jesus Christ of Nazareth, back in the midst of civilization. Jesus Christ of Nazareth is the only reason why we still have some sense of civility left on earth today! "And with him they crucify two thieves; the one on his right hand, and the other on his left. And the scripture was fulfilled, which said, and he was numbered with the transgressors (Mark 15: 27-28)." This was the final battle. Now all the three first born sons of God the Father were now being crucified. They were hanging from the tree of Life in the midst of the garden. The tree of Life now turned into the tree of death and hell. All because of the depth of sin now owed, by the actions and disobedience of the two sons of God the Father.

The tree that once represented life and civilization now became a tree, representing death and curses; instead of Life and prosperity, the same tree of Life in the midst of the garden. Civilization was about to be extinguish but, Jesus Christ of Nazareth was now placed in the midst of his two brothers "Jesus Christ/ Lucifer" and "Jesus/old Adamic nature". "Jesus Christ, Lucifer" still refusing to repent, but his brother "Jesus/old Adamic nature" realized he was guilty of trying to take the kingdom of God the Father by force. He repented while rebuking is brother "Jesus Christ, Lucifer" and found grace through Jesus Christ of Nazareth.

> Luke 23:39-43 tells us, "And one of the malefactors which were hanged railed on him, saying, if thou be Christ, save thyself and us.40 But the other answering rebuked him, saying, dost not thou fear God, seeing thou art in the same condemnation? 41 And we indeed justly; for we receive the due reward of our deeds: but this man hath done nothing amiss.42 And he said unto Jesus, Lord; remember me when thou comest into the kingdom. 43 And Jesus said unto him, "Verily I say unto thee, today shalt thou be with me in Paradise."

Chapter Ten

Repairing the Breach

To God Be The Glory, In the Mighty Name of Jesus Christ of Nazareth. Message: I was finally broken!

December 2004, I found myself detained at the Rollington Town Police Station. For the first time, I was finally broken! While sitting in a dimly lit, lonely room, I observed there were four chairs. I sat on one and pulled another directly in front of me. It was then, that I began to speak candidly with God. Instead of me doing all the talking, this time I was now listening. Many times, when we are talking to God, in our prayers, we are the ones doing all the talking. Isn't it a conversation? So, give God a chance to answer you. That morning, about 2:00am, Iris, the woman I was living with for years, my common law wife, came to the station to get me. You see, Iris was the reason I was at the Rollington Town Police Station.

One evening she came home from work, she was on the phone and began to put water on the stove. She used the bathroom and she was on her phone not realizing that I was home. I overheard her making plans to see another man, in our house. We both were cheating on each other while we were in this "committed relationship." As she realized that I was there, we began to argue about it. I became aggressive, I had a knap sack on my back and I

135

used it to hit her on the head. Iris reached for two kitchen towels, I realized what was about to happened, by this time her son was now approaching the kitchen, she yelled to him, "move Gracian," Gracian moved as Iris reached for the pot of boiling water that was on the stove. I recognized what was about to go down. As I turned around to get out of the way, it was too late; the boiling water covered my back. As I began to remove my shirt, my skin began to peel off unto my shirt, by this time I was holding unto Iris, yelling at her. "This is what you do to me after seven years?" I wanted to lick the hell out of her, but I found myself getting weak in my arms and I let her go. Was this divine intervention? I was standing there burning up, with a knife now in my hand, while holding the one who burned me. Was it God who remove the strength from my arms to save us both? When I let her go, she ran outside the house, and for some stupid reason, I rushed after her. As I reach outside the gate with the knife still in my hand, I could see two police men who were known to me. The officers shouted at me while reaching for their guns, it was then that I threw away the knife. One of the policemen walked up and gave me a slap in the face and immediately I fell onto the ground. The thing that hurt me the most out of the whole ordeal was not the burn that I had received, it wasn't the fact that I didn't get back at her. It was the fact that the police man who slapped me in the face was the one on the phone with Iris. He was the reason for the argument. I was taken to the police station, and a few hours later Iris arrived, I confronted her about the situation and the fact that the arresting officer was the reason for our fight. After our conversation, she told the officers that she didn't want to press any charges against me. When she left the station, I was now free but, I had nowhere to go!

Being so badly burned, one would think that the first place I should have gone was to the hospital to seek treatment. I went back to the house, I had to see her. I knocked on the door and few minutes later, I was inside, telling her I was sorry for my actions. While I was at the station, for the first time, I was convicted. I had made peace with God and we were now in a relationship. It is hard to admit your faults and become one with God, but when you get connected, you will never be the same again! I told Iris that I just wanted to sleep home for the night and I would leave in the morning. The next morning, I went straight to the Edna Manley Clinic on Grants Pen Road in Kingston for treatment.

I was now homeless, jobless and broke. I begged Iris to let me stay with her until I find somewhere. It was while heading back to Iris's home that evening, when I heard a man preaching. This man, I would later find out, was Bishop S who had been hired by the Harvest Army Church to preach during their crusade. I made my way to the church and I spoke with him. Later I understood after God had revealed it to me, this man, this Bishop S who God used to save me that day, was in fact a sorcerer. I tried to convey this to Bishop C who hired Bishop S to preach at the tent crusade. I told Bishop C that I was planning on speaking with Bishop S. It was then that Bishop C told me only a Bishop can correct a Bishop, only an Elder can correct another Elder, and I should keep quiet. After the crusade Bishop S was assigned to another church located in the Waltham Park Area to Pastor.

One Sunday morning during their annual convention, I attended Bishop S's church, it was during the worship service Bishop S began to speak to me over the microphone, "If God told you something about me, why didn't you confront me about it personally?" I tried to get to him and explain but his reply was, "too late." You see, I was not aware that Bishop C had been lying and manipulating the situation. Bishop C had gone back to Bishop S carrying bones, bones which I never gave him to carry. I later found out that Bishop S was kicked out of the church because of the information I had given to Bishop C. They were spiritually afraid of Bishop S because I told Bishop C, "physically you may be the one running this church, but spiritually Bishop S was in control." It's been years since this had happened and I never saw Bishop S again. I have been dealing with the guilt of how the situation transpired since 2005. It is my prayer that someday our paths will cross again, and the truth of the matter can be discussed. Who knows, I may gain another brother in Christ!

Wow, isn't it ironic, Bishop C would always tell me that Lucifer was the one speaking to me but as soon as it came to his business place (church), he was more than willing to believe me. Why didn't he use the same positive information to reach Bishop S, instead of pushing him away (firing him)? If all of that wasn't enough, while attending Bishop C's church, I became associated with one of his Deacons. This Deacon wasn't an older man, but he was considered one of the wise spiritual Elders of the church. After years of searching, God brought someone to me, who claimed that he knew exactly where I was inside the spiritual realm. We began praying together, he was now teaching me to take control over my own spirit and body. He began teaching me how to denounce evil demonic spirits, inside and around me, in the mighty name of Jesus Christ of Nazareth!

Jesus Christ of Nazareth, while he was on earth, taught us that no man can take control of a house, until he first binds up the strong man of the house. When we finish praying, we notice immediately that my actions, appearance, and even my voice sounded different. The spirit realm was now open to me! One day I ask Iris to marry me, but she refused. I was now attending church very regularly and I thought it was appropriate, since we had been living together for almost eight years. "You have nothing to give me," was her excuse. I spent time with God that night praying, before going to bed, then God spoke to me in a vision. In the vision I saw three women, when I asked God if Iris should be my wife, He said, "No." I ask him about Hyacinth who was now my prayer partner, He said, "No," then I ask him about the next person, in the vision, but God went silent. This was my first lesson as a young prophet, and I learned it the hardest way. My advice to all the young prophets and prophetesses out there is to remember you are God's mouth piece. When God speaks, then you speak. If He goes silent then you must go silent too. I began to tell people about my vision. Bishop C from the Harvest Army Church heard about it and started to address me from behind the pulpit. It was then I learned that the third woman in the vision was already married. I was the one still speaking, God had gone silent! Bishop C cursed me from behind the pulpit that Sunday, and guess what? He had every right to. I was so ashamed and confused. "The devil is the one showing you all those things," he shouted at me, in the form of preaching from the pulpit. "God wouldn't give you another man's wife." At first, I was angry, but he was right, I was the one lying on God, after God went silent, I too, should have gone silent. Bishop C taught me that Sunday one of the best lessons ever, speak when God speaks, go silent when He goes silent! Bishop C, today I have a great relationship with God, because of you sir! Thank you very much. I love you. It was while I was still attending the Harvest Army Church, that my spiritual cleansing started: all hell broke loose one Sunday, I was going through a cleansing process and those demons weren't giving up easily. The members of the church can attest to these claims. I had a vision of a woman! I later discovered that the same women that I saw in my vision, was in fact real, not just a vision, but assigned to me by Satan. *Did you know that when you are converted, immediately the devil assigns someone or something to befall you?* The woman I dreamed about invited me for dinner at her home. As I entered the yard I noticed that her head was wrapped in a piece of cloth. She began to confide in me that an evil spirit was living in her house. I immediately began to pray. The spirits living in the home were angry, so much so that the woman and her children ran from the house. I commanded those spirits, "in the name of JESUS CHRIST OF NAZARETH," to leave the house, they did. That night when we went back to church, she told Bishop C what happened. It was then that I learned they both had planned the whole thing. Bishop C wanted to see how I would behave around this woman in private; this was the same sister from my vision, earlier. "And he called them unto him, and said unto them in a parable, how can Satan cast out Satan. And if Satan rise up against himself, and be divided, he cannot stand, but have an end (Mark 3:23-27)." God used me, to give himself Glory! This woman was suffering with evil spirits for years; this part of the story was true, the church knew and couldn't help, but as soon as God intervened, my God. Bishop C said, "I was the prince of Persia, the evil spirits left only because, I was their commanding officer."

> Matthew 12:25-28 And Jesus knew their thoughts, and said unto them, Every Kingdom divided against itself is brought to desolation: and every city or house divided against itself shall not stand: 26 And if Satan cast out Satan, he is divided against himself; how shall then his kingdom stand? 27 And if I by Beelzebub cast out devils, by whom do your children cast them out? therefore they shall be your

141

> judges. 28 But if I cast out devils by the Spirit of
> God, then the kingdom of God is come unto you.

After spending about two years worshipping with bishop C, they decided that it was now time for me to leave their church. One Sunday night during worship service, they called the police to remove me from the church, according to them I was possessed. I was so confused, about people who call themselves Christians, yet harbor malice and claim that they are on their way to heaven. For years this would affect me negatively, until *God revealed to me that there are three (3) churches upon the earth. Satan also has his places of worship and his own worshippers too, who call themselves Christians*. "Behold, I will make them of the synagogue of Satan, which say they are Jews, and are not, but do lie; behold, I will make them to come and worship before your feet, and to know that I have loved thee (Revelation 3:9)." Many will profess that they have a good relationship with God! These same people find it hard to forgive their brothers or sisters who may have offended them. These self-righteous people would hand you a one-way ticket to hell, without a chance to redeem yourself. I pray that God will soon reveal himself to these self-righteous fools! How can you hate your brothers or sisters while professing, that you love, or even know God? "He that loved not knoweth not God; for God is love. No man hath seen God at any time, if we love one another, God dwelled in us, and his love is made perfected in us (1 John 4: 8.)" I hear you in the spirit as you read saying, "But he was the one who did me wrong!" "Yes, he did, but did he or she ask to be forgiven?" If your answer is yes, then your duty is to forgive, this is what Jesus Christ of Nazareth taught us all while he was on earth. We are to forgive each other, but if we fail to forgive each other, even so our Heavenly father won't forgive us. Be careful with that spirit of self-righteousness, you are transforming into a witch, wizard or sorcerer. How do you know? Years ago, the same thing happened to me. I got a second chance to make it right, and I did! I implore you to do the same before it's too late! In order for me to receive my spiritual deliverance, I had to first forgive bishop C, and "Free Myself" from the prison of Unforgiveness! "No man can enter into a strong man's house, and spoil his goods, except he will first bind the strong man; and then he will spoil his house (Mark 3:27)." One Sunday the Deacons gave me a book to read called, "*The Fourth Dimension,*" as he received all his information from this spiritual book. God was now using another sorcerer to set me free from my spiritual prison. This book that he gave me to read was about spiritualism. As I read the introduction, then chapter one, my brain went blank. That night God spoke to me for the first time, in a vision, revealing to me, do not read that book. I went to church the following Sunday, and told the Deacon that God told me not to read any more of that book. He then told me it was the demons stopping me from reading it, because they wanted to keep me bound.

I brought the book back home to read but, when I opened the book, my brain went blank (dead) again. God shut down my brain system, in-order to protect me, he wanted to deliver me. I was now trying the spirit, each time I put down that book, I would read the Bible. My brain was alive, but as soon as I opened that book, my brain went back blank again. This was all the proof that I needed, God was the one speaking to me all this time. To this day, the Deacon still believes I have not been delivered, because I didn't read his book. There will always be others in this world, who will try to keep us in bondage, after all God himself set us free. That night, while I was praying and calling on the name of Jesus Christ, *my version of Jesus Christ also showed up*. It was then I saw all sorts of creeping things, inside the room coming towards me. I remembered what the Deacon taught me, and I began to shout, "Not this Jesus Christ, I want JESUS CHRIST OF NAZARETH." That was when all hell broke loose inside that house, the creeping things started scattering (running) up and down, then there was a loud noise as if the roof was caving in. The tie between hell and I was now broken! I was not delivered but, the covenant that I entered with Satan fifteen years ago, was now broken. There is no greater power than Jesus Christ of Nazareth! I dare you to put God in control! Over the years I have experienced many things in this Christian life. I have been put out of churches, by well know Bishops and Pastors in Jamaica. They even used the police to throw me out of their churches, even threaten me with a restraining order, to bar me from entering their premises or congregations. 1 Corinthians 6:1, "Dare any of you, having a matter against another, go to law before the unrighteous, and not before the saints? God is the force, to defend him." It was this incident that He taught me that there are three churches upon the earth today. Revelation 3:9, "Indeed I will make them of the synagogue of Satan, which say they are Jews, and are not, but do lie; behold, I will make them come and worship before thy feet, and to know that I have loved thee." Over the years, men have made their own churches, and given themselves all types of names and titles. **Now we have three churches:**

(1) One belongs to God:

(1) One belongs to Satan:

(1) One belongs to man.

Let us all be mindful, before we start to curse and place labels on the church. Find out first who owns the church that you are talking about. I have received many questions from brothers and sisters of the faith, asking me why is it that "People who call themselves Christians, are not dressing holy?" You and I, only belong to God, whenever we do what He commands us to do. To those of you who are reading this book and to those brothers and sisters who sent me messages on Facebook posts, understand this, you are giving them too much of your time, please, do not let them transform you. When I was facing my trials, I could have chosen to become a (vegetable Christian) or an (egg Christian). The egg Christians, are those that are nice, warm, gentle, and very promising. But as soon as they are put in boiling water (facing trials), they suddenly get hard (mean and bitter) and lose their true purpose in life. Vegetable Christians are those that have nothing to be desired at first, they are rough and dirty (mean and bitter) but when washed (by the blood of Jesus Christ of Nazareth) and put into boiling water (facing trials), they get soft (Christ like)!

Question: Whose church are you a member of? This message is not for everyone, but for those who were given assignments from God in the past, and for those chosen new converts, who God had given new assignments. If you believed, that God saved you for a reason and had given you a purpose, or work, pay careful attention to this paragraph, it yours!

First thing you need to know and understand is that *there are laws, and rules that govern the spiritual realm.* **The second** thing you need to know and understand is these laws and rules must be kept, and followed, if not then the body of Christ will be destroyed. Even worse, they can even become spiritually Luke-warm or spiritually stagnant. **Finally, the third thing** you must know and understand is that Satan also knows these laws too. Therefore, he was bright enough to confront God. Why? Satan knows that God cannot lie, he also knows, that God cannot go back on his word. When God met him, inside the church, raising havoc, Satan simply repeat back these laws to God, and reminded God of His own rules of the spiritual realms, this is found in Mark 1:24 saying, "Let us alone, what have we to do with thee, thou Jesus Christ of Nazareth? Art thou come to destroy us? I know thee, who thou art,

146

the Holy One of God." "Leave us alone; what was Satan really telling Jesus Christ of Nazareth?" Answer: I was comfortable living in this church until you came; these leaders are my bosom friends and associates. But you have come and disturb me, I still refused to repent, and you cannot force me: furthermore it is not time yet for my punishment: remember that you have given me time to reign over the earth, and I have not reign yet; God, are you going back on your own words? I know exactly who you are; you are God inside the flesh of Jesus Christ of Nazareth. You are the light of this world: and light cannot mix up with darkness: so (just leave me alone). Can two walk together, except they be agreed? (Amos 3:3) I did not add to the words of God, nor did I take away from His word, I simple revealed the Truth. I told you before that this message is not for everyone!

Break-forth now elect of God, all those with a purpose or having assignments given to you by God. We are about to open, your spiritual prison and set you free, in the name of Jesus Christ of Nazareth: Satan did not put you (us) there in your spiritual prison, (disobedience and lack of God knowledge) did. We are the ones who sometime lacked ourselves in this spiritual prison, by not knowing these rules of the spirit realm. But the worst part of all of this is: you and I had the key all those years while sitting in prison, "the name of Jesus Christ of Nazareth" is not only a saving name, but the "Key" to the third dimension in Heaven, Earth and Hell. For "The elect to be fully prepared and operate the "Key" (the

147

name of Jesus Christ of Nazareth) effectively, we "must" be living daily in Repentance (Matthew 16:19). And I will give unto thee the keys of the kingdom of heaven: and whatsoever thou shalt bind on earth shall be bound in heaven; and whatsoever thou shalt loose on earth shall be loosed in heaven. God's promises can only be done unto us, if we know our rights and keeps these rules and regulations of the Spiritual realm, in the name of Jesus Christ of Nazareth: Each Christian, should be cleansing themselves before God, daily, I will even go as far to say, not hour by hour or minute by minutes, but second by second! "And when he had called unto him his twelve disciples, he gave them power against unclean spirits, to cast them out, and to heal all manner of sickness and all manner of disease. (Matthew 10:1)" Hyacinth, my young prayer partner, and I were praying for a woman one day who was possessed with an evil spirit. The woman was displaying two different personalities, at one point you could heard her crying for help. Then a harsh voice spoke, "Leave me alone, I know you, and if you ever backslide, I will kill you," the voice kept repeating, "I will kill you." I began to pray aloud, "Spirits of darkness in the name of JESUS CHRIST OF NAZARETH, I command you to get out, and do not returned." The spirits refused to leave. I continued in prayer, "in the name of JESUS CHRIST OF NAZARETH, what is your name?" The voice replied, "My name is f----." Why are you here? "I am here that she will walk and f---- everyone she meets." I decreed, "in the name of JESUS CHRIST OF

148

NAZARETH, I rebuke you and send you back to the pit of hell."

Remember This: Whenever you are casting out a demon, and he refuses to leave, that demon was placed there by someone or something. The demon left but returned three times before I realized that she was wearing something that was attracting the demons. It was then I stepped out of the room, ask the young woman to remove all clothing and jewelry and replaced the clothing with new garments. After she was dressed in her new garments, I stood flatfooted in front of her. She was crying and afraid, even a bit angry. I knew I had been warring for her soul. I began to speak with authority, "I will stand to bear witnesses against you, and I will judge you on judgment day, in the name of JESUS CHRIST OF NAZARETH, get out and do not returned." This time we heard a loud cry and the spirits left. God is still teaching me every day, I am learning something new daily. God was delivering me from the spirit of witchcraft, while teaching me the power of his name, yes, the mighty name of JESUS CHRIST OF NAZARETH.

"Wherefore God also hath highly exalted him and given him a name which is above every name; That at the name of Jesus every knee shall bow, of things in heaven, and things in earth, and things under the earth (Philippians 2: 9-10)."

Chapter Eleven

Deliverance

To God Be The Glory, In the Name of Jesus Christ of Nazareth. Now Unto the Chosen of God Message: Deliverance Is Done in Three Steps: Instantly, Short-term, and Long-term.

When I just got baptized, about twenty years ago, a sex demon held me into captivities for years. Yet I was professing that I was saved and what made it worst was the fact that I would still felt the presence of the Holy Spirit. Yes, we all have our weaknesses, and sometimes they are in different areas of our lives, but none of us are immune from trials and temptations.

To God be all the glory, in the name of Jesus Christ of Nazareth. Today I can proudly testify that I have overcome these sex demon spirits and fully delivered. But once it wasn't like this, my God: I was so defenseless against these sex demons that at the time seems to control my life. I was really struggling with these sex spirits that was manifesting itself through the form of Masturbations. For hours each day, I would be playing around with myself until my fleshy desire was being satisfied, but why was this happening to me? 1 Corinthians 3:16 Know you not that you are the temple of God, and that the Spirit of God dwelleth in you? 17 If any man defile the temple of God, him shall God destroy; for the temple of God is Holy, which temple you are.

150

Deliverance

Even though I was professing Christianity, I was still doing my own thing, watching adult movies, and reading all sorts of adult magazines.

Then one day, I came across Proverbs 23:7 For as he thinketh in his heart, so is he: Eat and drink, saith he to thee; but his heart is not with thee. Wow, knowledge is powerful. That same day I learned this was in the Bible and accept it: that was it, each day I would tell my own spirit, enough is enough, in the name of Jesus Christ of Nazareth, my God, I had the power to stop all along but I just need a different mindsets, and the name of Jesus Christ of Nazareth. The reason for this personal confession is simple: just to encourage someone who maybe struggling with these demonic spirits or any other demonic spirits assign to you.

For all those new converts joining the "team" or any individuals who are still struggling, with these sex demons or any other spirits, keep encouraging yourself that you are going to make it, in the name of Jesus Christ of Nazareth. You will make it, I did, all because I refused to let God go, wow, though it took me almost a lifetime, I am fully mature now spiritually. Today, I am giving God all the glory, In the name of Jesus Christ of Nazareth, thanking Him for not giving up on me, even when I gave upon my own self. My life now brings God glory and honor through the name of His only begotten Son Jesus Christ of Nazareth.

Now based, upon my own personal deliverance processes, I have learned that deliverance can be done in three steps: *Instantly, Short term, and Long term.*

Over the years, I have experienced all three deliverance processes. That night, while in the detention room in the police station, I formed a personal relationship with God, who visited me and "Instantly Delivered" my soul from the pit of "Hell," and delivering me from the spirits of hatred, I once had for Him. I was so angry with God, and for twelve long years, I Spair Lee, refused to call upon God and His righteousness. Isn't it ironic that most of us only seem to know or remember God, when our back is against the wall? Well, I was no different, all my friends and family members that I contacted refused to help, WOW, isn't it ironic how many of our associates seems to be there for us: until we are sick or in need of help. For the first time in twelve years, I finally figure it out, that I was all on my own. When reality came in: I was now totally broken, for the first time in my life I felt so defenseless: I honestly didn't know what to do or who to call. Then I started to pray unto God or should I say start cursing God. How could a loving God cause me to be going through all of this? I didn't realize at that time, it was all because of my disobedience and very poor choices I had made. Here I was venting my anger and arguing with God: Then I felt as if someone was hugging me, there was a peace inside my soul even though I was still hand-cuffed to the window grill, I felt so free, I was now experiencing

Deliverance

an "Instant Deliverance process" God saved me from my "own-self". When I was set free of all those charges, immediately, I got baptized and start to attend church regularly, now that I am exposed to the light of Jesus Christ of Nazareth. I started to notice all my old bad habits more clearly, I thought after being baptized, that I would automatically drop off everything all at once. But this is not so, those bad habits will all go little by little, the more you grow spiritually, the faster they go. Not all at once, but gradually. What can wash away my sins, nothing but the blood of Jesus Christ of Nazareth?

I have baptized over again in the name of our Lord Jesus Christ of Nazareth: more than thirteen (13) years now, and I am still struggling daily to live clean and Holy unto God: Until I "Found the secret of living for God" what? "Surrendering totally unto God," living for God becomes difficult and hard when we refuse to change from our own "Selfishness and Pride"! This did not come overnight; it took me quite some time to learn how to walk into righteousness. Today, I am still failing him repeatedly: but love and mercies refuses to let me go astray; and I refused to quit or give up: in the name of Jesus Christ of Nazareth.

Few weeks after my personal encounter with God: I was praying one night using the name title of Jesus Christ, and Jesus, then the spirits of the Anti-Christ came back to me: No! I shouted out, no not this Jesus: I need Jesus Christ of Nazareth: I was now experiencing my "Short termDeliverance". While I was praying

153

that night, I remember seeing all sorts of creeping things coming to me, lizards, black birds and cats, my God! No not these Jesuses I cried, "I need Jesus Christ of Nazareth," immediately the covenant between me and hell was being broken: but I wasn't fully being delivered.

> Romans 1:18-32, tells us , For the wrath of God is revealed from heaven against all ungodliness and unrighteousness of men, who hold the truth in unrighteousness; 19 Because that which may be known of God is manifest in them; for God hath shewed it unto them. 20 For the invisible things of him from the creation of the worked are clearly seen being understood by the things that are made, even his eternal power and Godhead; so that they are without excuse: 21 Because that, when they knew God, they glorified him not as God, neither were thankful; but became vain in their imaginations, and their foolish heart was darkened. 22 Professing themselves to be wise, they became fools. 23 And changed the glory of the incorruptible God into an image mad like to corruptible man, and to birds, and four-footed beasts, and creeping things. 24 Wherefore God also gave them up to uncleanness through the lust of their own hearts, to dishonor their own bodies between themselves; 25 Who change the truth of God into a lie, and worshipped and served the creature more than the Creator, who is blessed forever. Amen.26 For this cause God gave them up unto vile affections: For even their women did change the natural use into that which is against nature: 27 And likewise also the men, leaving the natural use of the woman, burned in their lust one toward another; men with men working that which is unseemly, and receiving in themselves that recompense of their error which

was meet. 28 And even as they did not like to retain God in their knowledge, God gave them over to a reprobate mind, to do those things which are not convenient; 29 Being filled with all unrighteousness, fornication, wickedness, covetousness, maliciousness; full of envy, murder, debate, deceit, malignity; whisperers. 30 Backbiters, haters of God, despiteful, proud, boaster, inventors of evil things, disobedient to parents, 31 Without understanding, covenant breakers, without natural affection , implacable, unmerciful: 32 Who knowing the judgment of God, that thy which commit such things are worthy of death, not only do the same, but have pleasure in them that do them.

To God Be The Glory, In the Name of Jesus Christ of Nazareth:

Now Unto The Churches

Message: The Best Things Are Always Free!

Did you know that the best gifts are always free? Humans over the years have always tried to pay for these things, even though they were freely given to us by God.   Understand that from the beginning of our fore-parents Adam and Eve, They were given a beautiful home by Almighty God: they SOLD their home along with their spiritual birth right, to Satan for a false hope and empty promises. They then turned around paying rent for the home they once own: in "Pain and Suffering" when all along it was FREE. God gave humans, Free Will to choose our own destiny, but we SOLD this also to Satan, for Greediness, Selfishness, Hatred.

Genesis 4:3 and in process of time it came to pass,
that Cain brought of the fruit of the ground an
offering unto the LORD. 4 And Abel also brought
of the firstlings of his flock and of the fat thereof.
And the LORD Had respect unto Abel and to his
offering.

When God ask Cain and Abel to make an offering this was not forced it was all Free Will. Cain chooses to sell his FREEDOM to Satan for envy and selfish condemnation. It was clear that Cain had begun suffering and paying for the things he once owned for FREE! Today it is no different, God gave unto us "Free Salvation" and yet the human family would still rather pay for it: through long fasting rituals when all that is required were already paid for, when God place upon Jesus Christ of Nazareth our sins. Now as Sinners, all we are required to do is believe and accept Jesus Christ of Nazareth: as our personal savior and we receive God's Free Gift of eternal life. Humanity has rejected this Free Gift and chose to pay for it. How? Humanity continues to sew monetary seeds into manmade ministries and starve themselves as they fast. All God required from you and I, are faith and a true confessed heart: Then open our arms and just accept Jesus Christ of Nazareth. **Leviticus 1: 3 says, "If his offering be a burnt sacrifice of the herd, let him offer a male without blemish: he shall offer it at door of the Tabernacle of the congregation before the LORD."**

To God be all the glory in the name of Jesus Christ of Nazareth: Message: The curses were finally broken: God removed the spirits of witchcraft and curses from off my life. After being evicted from almost all those churches that I had attended in the Kingston area: sometimes by using the police or the Bishops or Pastors would just ask me to leave, looking back now, my God: I have to just smile, I remember there were times when I refused to leave or not leaving fast enough: They would "Physically hold me and put me outside of their churches":

I was now finally broken and confused; all hope seems lost: In January 2012, I was invited back to the same church that first introduce me to the spiritual realm: One Sunday morning during worship, I heard the bishop saying that he needed spiritual help, well I thought that it was a turning point in his life: but this man was seeking God in the wrong places. Psalm 1:1 Blessed is the man that walketh not in the counsel of the ungodly, nor stand in the way of sinners, nor sitteth in the seat of the scornful.

After the death of the two witches who he was working with, the familiar spirit's that was working with them refuses to work with him, but why? The spirits that they were using while they were alive: now refusing to work with him: They didn't find favor with him: He had already out grown those familiar spirits; but he did not know that. It was now time for him to come face to face with Jesus Christ of Nazareth! He sought the assistance of two other witches in a place called Papine. That Sunday morning during worship service, I could hear the chanting of both witches that he invited: They were both sitting down behind me; Few minutes later, the spiritual ritual started: "Hell No" I shouted, you

157

are not going to work obeah "sorcery" in front of me today. The Bishop and Pastor were telling me to be quiet: "Hell No" not in front of me I repeated, I got up and went over to where they had placed a red candle on the floor inside the church. I took up the candle and broke it in pieces. The Bishop went back to the altar they have in the church and remove another red candle: I stood still in a bid to wait until he placed it back on the floor, then I removed it and broke it up into pieces and throw them outside. It is possible that God was the one who allowed me to come back to this church: When I meet God in the police station that night; I had asked Him if I should go back to this church. He told me No! Seven years later, He led me back there, but why? Yes! To do my final exam: What Spair Lee?

When I was fourteen years old, this is the same church that I was filled in: What explain? One Friday night during young people service, while I was moderating the worship service: I ask everyone in the church to stand up: Then I turned my eyes toward Heaven and ask God to pour out all His Power on me: I requested that He gave me everything: I was out: I really can't remember for how long: But when I came back to reality; I find myself holding on to the pulpit, and all I can remember inside is: You asked me to pour out everything: I didn't even pour out, and you are not able to contain me! But when God Reveal Himself unto me: I didn't know Him personally and that is how I ended up being a Sorcerer: And right inside of this church too! At fourteen years old, I didn't know

Him personally and those people who lead me to Him: They didn't know Him personally either, I didn't have a chance then; But when I finally figure out and came to myself! God brought me back to "Resist My Final Spiritual Exam": God will never " Charge us for someone else's mistake" that is why I was able to "Resist" or resist!

It was then I remembered the vision that I had the previous night! In this vision I was told to hug the Bishop and his wife: Then in that same vision: I was instructed to let them go. I hugged both, the bishop was resisting; but I held unto him as he shouted, you are a madman; Then I left their church! That Monday morning while praying alone and questioning God: I was now broken and confused, God! I shouted: I didn't care who was hearing me: haven't I suffered long enough now? Please God, I beg you, in the name of Jesus Christ of Nazareth, with tears streaming out of my eyes and a heavy heart. I cried: God please, I'd rather die: than to continue living with these spirits of witchcrafts any longer. I had already spent a total of twenty-two years, living in the spirits of witchcraft: I was tired, burden down and weary. I felt when God moved, and a heavy weight lifted off me, my God! I was so excited that immediately, I fell to the floor giving God thanks and praises. My God, I thank you in the name of Jesus Christ of Nazareth.

After "seven long years", the curses were now finally removed: By God Himself, in the name of Jesus Christ of Nazareth. God had kept His promise with me! What do you mean Spair? December 2004/ I got saved while in that police station. After I was set free, I tried to sign up for a Biblical school: The teacher was trying to explain Exodus 33:23 And I will take away mine hand, and thou shalt see my back parts: but my face shall not be seen. She was now telling me that God was showing Moses from his waist to his bottom: garbage, that night I went home and while there praying: I asked God are you a homosexual God, why did this woman said that you show Moses your Ass! Immediately! In a vision that night I SpairLee was instructed to stop going to Bible class! "I will teach you what I God want you to know and I God will Deliver you Myself!!! This is the reason why I cannot and will not be subjected unto any Man! "Until they are representing the same kingdom that I Spair Lee is Representing." To God be all the glory in the name of Jesus Christ of Nazareth.

Psalms 139:7-8 Whither shall I go from thy Spirit? or whither shall I flee from thy presence? 8 If I ascend up into Heaven, Thou art there: If I make my bed in hell, Behold thou art there. For the pass twenty-two years, I had been living in the pit of "Hell" but today I am thanking God for the blood of the Lamb and the name of Jesus Christ of Nazareth: Today I am totally delivered and set free! I am now reaching out to others, who are either in ""Hell" or those who are on their way into hell: To God be all the glory in the name of Jesus Christ of Nazareth. One day while I was praying, God! I know that you have saved and change my life:

160

But before you came in, I was using all sorts of things: believing I was doing your work! What should I use now God? This was a very important question: Why? Before I got saved: I was working with water, Olive oils, Florida water and others stuff, bathing people with bushes given to me by demonic spirits! That night I got a vision, in this vision someone was speaking with me: All you need now is the name of "Jesus Christ of Nazareth": My God, for about seven days: Every night I got the same vision, all you need is my name: The name of "Jesus Christ of Nazareth". Today, when I am worshipping, I find myself shouting a lot, at first I was concerned: until I read Joshua 6:20, So the people shouted when the priests blew with the trumpets: and it came to pass, when the people heard the sound of the trumpet, and the people shouted with a great shout, that the wall fell down flat, so that the people went up into the city, every man straight before him, and they took the city. If I happen to be in your presence worshipping and you hear me shouting: If you have a personal problem with it; chances are, your Jericho wall needs to come down: in the name of "Jesus Christ of Nazareth". To God be all the glory in the name of "Jesus Christ of Nazareth:

Chapter Twelve

Prayer

To God Be The Glory,
In the Name of Jesus Christ of Nazareth:
Now Unto To Those Who Hunger for Deliverance!
Message: Prayer that the Holy Spirit Taught Me

This is a Deliverance prayer that God taught me through "The Holy Spirit." Each time I pray this prayer it keeps me out of the spirit realms where God doesn't want me, and it keeps me spiritually clean. Today I can defeat the whole army of Satan, while paralyzing the pit of hell, praying in the name of "Jesus Christ of Nazareth!!" This prayer is also a spiritual warfare armor, whenever a believing Christian prayed in this same sequence. *They will immediately* access audience in the presence of Almighty God Himself. Worshipping will become easier and burdens are broken in the name of Jesus Christ of Nazareth. Whenever Christians prayed, calling upon the name of Jesus Christ of Nazareth, we automatically closed the pit of hell, while being protected from Satan and all his Hosts of demons - To God be all the glory, in the name of Jesus Christ of Nazareth. Today, I must be constantly living in repentance and rebuking demons daily. Why? Those evil spirits come back to visit me regularly, but why? This is also biblical, Jesus Christ of Nazareth taught us saying:

Prayer

Matthew 12:43-45 When the unclean spirit is gone
out of a man, he walketh through dry places,
seeking rest, and findeth none. 44 Then he saith, I
will return into my house from whence I came out;
and when he is come, he findeth it empty, swept,
and garnished. 45 Then forth he, and taketh with
himself seven other spirits more wicked than
himself, and they enter in and dwell there: and the
last state of that man is worse than the first. Even so
shall it be also unto this wicked generation.

This prayer is only an example of how we should address our prayers unto God: in the name of Jesus Christ of Nazareth, while using your own words in the future.

LET US PRAY

Father, in the name of JESUS CHRIST OF NAZARETH, I humble myself before you. God wash me and cleanse in the blood of JESUS CHRIST OF NAZARETH.

Father, I surrender everything to you now in the name of JESUS CHRIST OF NAZARETH. My heart, my mind, my body, and my soul, in the name of JESUS CHRIST OF NAZARETH. Let your divine presence keep me in your will, in the name of JESUS CHRIST OF NAZARETH.

Spirit of darkness inside and around me, in the name of JESUS CHRIST OF NAZARETH, I rebuke you from my presence, you have no power over me, in the name of JESUS CHRIST OF NAZARETH. I refuse your influences over my life in the name of JESUS CHRIST OF NAZARETH.

Inspired by God

Father, in the name of JESUS CHRIST OF NAZARETH, God I am no match for the devil; but you are, in the name of JESUS CHRIST OF NAZARETH. Fight on my behalf, I beseech you; keep me in your presence in the name of JESUS CHRIST OF Nazareth. Amen.

Prayer

Notes

Notes

www.ingramcontent.com/pod-product-compliance
Lightning Source LLC
Chambersburg PA
CBHW060926040426
42445CB00011B/813